CRIME

AND ITS

VICTIMS

DANIEL W. VAN NESS

 foreword by
Charles W. Colson

*Including Study Questions for
Individuals or Groups*

INTERVARSITY PRESS
DOWNERS GROVE, ILLINOIS 60515

FLORIDA
CHRISTIAN
COLLEGE
LIBRARY

InterVarsity Press is the book-publishing division of Inter-Varsity Christian Fellowship, a student movement active on campus at hundreds of universities, colleges and schools of nursing. For information about local and regional activities, write IVCF, 233 Langdon St., Madison, WI 53703.

Distributed in Canada through InterVarsity Press, 860 Denison St., Unit 3, Markham, Ontario L3R 4H1, Canada.

All Scripture quotations, unless otherwise indicated, are from the Holy Bible, New International Version. Copyright © 1973, 1978, International Bible Society. Used by permission of Zondervan Bible Publishers.

Cover illustration: Ed Sobieraj

ISBN 0-87784-512-3

Printed in the United States of America

Library of Congress Cataloging in Publication Data

Van Ness, Daniel W., 1949-
  Crime and its victims.

  (Impact books)
  Bibliography: p.
  Includes index.
  1. Victims of crimes—United States. 2. Criminal justice, Administration of—United States.
3. Punishment—Religious aspects—Christianity. 4. Crime prevention—United States. I. Title.
HV6250.3.U5V36   1986   362.8'8'0973   86-10467
ISBN 0-87784-512-3

17	16	15	14	13	12	11	10	9	8	7	6	5	4	3	2
99	98	97	96	95	94	93	92	91	90	89	88	87	86		

Impact Books

Making an impact on your world.

Christians are to be in the world but not of it. We are to change the world, not let it change us. Yet there are many forces seeking to mold our Christianity to secular values. How can we live out the transforming power of the gospel and have an impact on our world?

Impact Books offer a Christian perspective on the major trends shaping our lives. They reveal how the truths of Scripture still hold the best hope for humanity in our rapidly changing society. Written by people who know their fields, Impact Books give practical suggestions for how Christianity can make a difference in you and your world.

Upcoming volumes will look at a number of significant influences on our lives, including computers, cultural values and changing sexual roles.

To Charles and Marjorie Van Ness

Foreword

Consider the statistics: there is a one-in-four chance that you, or someone in your household, will become a victim of crime within the next twelve months. If you live in San Francisco or Miami, your chances of being a victim of violent crime are one in twelve. You are safer driving in the Indianapolis 500 than walking the streets of most major American cities.

But even if you aren't a victim of crime in the coming year, you can't escape being victimized as a taxpayer. Budget-busting prison construction—more than seven billion dollars' worth—is breaking many states in a vain attempt to relieve overcrowded prisons. Repeat offenders soak up millions each year in court costs and lost wages. Meanwhile the prison population is growing ten times faster than the regular population.

So crime affects each of us—in its terrible impact on us or those we love, or in its insatiable drain on our pocketbooks. Unless checked, it will shred the fabric of our culture. Once order is broken down in a society, the biblical basis for government is destroyed.

Surprisingly enough, the atmosphere that allows crime to flourish begins with you and me: it's the widespread attitude that crime is a problem we can do nothing about. We have been led to believe that crime is somehow the business of police chiefs and FBI agents, politicians, sociologists and Hollywood producers. So we just sit back and watch the evening news unfold, growing more angry and frustrated.

This feeling of impotence is a dangerous illusion. In truth, the only people who really *can* do something about the crime and prison plague are ordinary citizens like you and me.

Government can't solve the prison gridlock. I saw why when I spent seven months behind bars after Watergate. Men lay day after day on their bunks, bitter, angry, bored, often forgotten by their families. Many simply passed their time plotting how they were going to get even when they got out of prison.

It's clear that prisons don't rehabilitate. In fact, one FBI study reveals that three out of four ex-offenders commit new crimes. But, as those of us who are Christians know, the reason government can't stop crime is that crime is not an institutional problem. At its root, crime is a spiritual malaise, the result of individuals making wrong moral choices. It is a matter of the heart and can be solved only when we apply moral solutions.

That's why I'm so excited about Dan's book. Dan and I have worked closely together for the past five years. We have walked prison cellblocks; we've met with political leaders at every level of government; we've studied and wrestled with the complex problems of criminal justice reform. Thus the contents of the pages which follow flow not only from thoughtful research, but from our experiences over the history of our ministry. Dan's book is a unique blend of these experiences, the keen insights of a finely trained legal mind—and the compassion of a committed Christian heart.

So I hope you will not only read this book, but pass it along to a friend or two. This is the first work I've read that offers practical, helpful insights, written from the perspective not only of prisoners and offenders but victims as well. As individuals, we *can* make a difference. We all have the responsibility to penetrate the heart of the problem. For Christians, that means: bringing Jesus Christ into the prisons, where his love can transform hardened criminals into committed disciples; applying practical, biblical solutions like restitution to the criminal justice problem; and bringing the gospel to bear on the spiritual cancers infecting our society as a whole.

Of course, if we ignore the message of this book and cloister ourselves, relegating the solution of crime to government, we'll see dramatic results of another kind: more and bigger prisons, larger police forces—and, as the evidence of recent decades so powerfully demonstrates, more and more crime.

In short, the beginning of a responsible and longlasting solution lies with you and me. Understanding how and where to begin lies in this marvelously insightful and readable book.

Charles W. Colson

Preface

In February 1980 a group of Christians met outside Washington, D.C., for a day and a half of meetings on the criminal justice system. Only days earlier the state prison at Santa Fe, New Mexico, had been torn by one of the bloodiest riots in history, leaving twenty-five dead and scores injured.

Chuck Colson had invited key Christian leaders in politics, law, the judiciary, corrections and social outreach to the strategy session. "After four years of working in prisons," he said, opening the meeting, "I am seeing the urgent need for criminal justice reform."

The group agreed. Prison overcrowding had created a crisis situation not only in New Mexico, but in virtually every state in the country. Most Christians were unaware of the problem. In fact, most supported "tougher" sentencing policies not realizing that these policies often aggravated overcrowding and did not reduce crime rates. Aware of that public opinion, officials faced the dilemma of appearing soft on crime or neglecting reasonable change.

There was a critical need for developing a response which conservative Christians could support. This response needed to be practical as well as theoretical. It needed to offer meaningful, realistic steps for political leaders. Education of the general public was crucial.

Shortly after this I joined Prison Fellowship—the ministry to prisoners, ex-prisoners and their families which Colson had formed in 1976. My job was to provide staff assistance to support the growing interest in this issue among public officials, the news media and the Christian community.

We produced the position paper *Is There a Better Way?* which outlined the problem and recommended reforms. Response was immediate. Legislators in Washington State, concerned over conditions in their maximum security prison at Walla Walla, asked for help in reforming their sentencing laws and revamping their correctional system. The chairman of the Senate Judiciary Committee in Indiana requested copies to distribute to every member of the legislature and asked for help in creating both a legislative response to that state's crisis and public support for the reforms. United States Senators Sam Nunn (D-Ga) and William Armstrong (R-Co) asked for help in creating federal policies that would ease the overcrowding in federal prisons without endangering public safety.

Public support also began to grow. Political commentators William F. Buckley, Paul Harvey, Jeff Hart, Mike McManus, William Raspberry and others became enthusiastic about using restitution and community service punishments instead of prison for nonviolent offenders.

In 1983 Prison Fellowship created an affiliate organization, Justice Fellowship, to support this growing interest and activity in criminal justice reform. Through research, public advocacy and grassroots networking, Justice Fellowship seeks to bring about criminal justice reforms which are consistent with biblical teaching on justice and righteousness.

We have come to see that the problems are much broader than the crisis in our prisons, although that crisis must be resolved. We have become increasingly concerned with the disservice that is done to victims of crime by the system itself. And we have become convinced that both problems stem from the same root: the modern view that crime is principally an offense by the criminal against the state.

What is presented in the following pages is what Justice Fellowship has learned in the past five years. It reflects our research, our growing understanding of how biblical teaching addresses the problem, and the insights of corrections professionals, criminal justice practitioners, victims, prisoners and biblical scholars.

Many people have helped me with this project. I acknowledge their contributions with gratitude. A few merit special thanks.

I began this project at the suggestion of Joan Lloyd Guest of Inter-Varsity Press. She has been an ideal editor, offering encouragement, ideas, skilled criticism and enthusiasm. She has become a good friend. Jack Stewart also provided excellent editorial assistance, and his suggestions have greatly improved my understanding of how biblical teaching can apply to our twentieth-century criminal justice concerns.

The Board of Justice Fellowship gave me time and encouragement to undertake this project. The staff of Justice Fellowship helped mind the shop while I disappeared to the library or word processor. David Coolidge provided ideas, research, commentary and encouragement. Elizabeth Leahy, Lisa Barnes, Glen Holley and Barbara Bird helped research, edit and type. James Copland compiled the indexes. The following scholars and friends reviewed earlier drafts and provided invaluable suggestions: Charles Babcock, Robert F. Cochran, Jr., Charles W. Colson, Cole Durham, Carl F. H. Henry, Robert Hubbard, David Larson, Millard Lind, Art Lindsley, Gordon Loux, Adah Moulton, Ronald Nikkel, Jean Sargent, James W. Skillen, Curran Tiffany and Michael Woodruff. I am greatly in their debt for this help.

Finally, I offer two special words of thanks. My wife, Brenda, has provided encouragement, support and forbearance during this project and has endured a distracted husband, lost vacations and interrupted holidays with good grace. And the Sargent/Van Ness Shepherd Group of Truro Episcopal Church has sustained this whole endeavor with prayer.

If victims, offenders and those working with them received the kind of support and help that I have enjoyed during this project, the effects of crime would certainly be reduced, and our society would be a more peaceful place to live.

Part I

What's Happening Here?

Chapter 1

Victims

Like most people, I thought I understood crime. Then on Monday, 15 November 1976, I came home to discover that our apartment door had been kicked in, our home ransacked and our property stolen.

Fortunately no one was there at the time, so no one was hurt. As crimes go it wasn't very spectacular. The police, who arrived an hour after we called them, were not even interested in coming upstairs to see the damage to our apartment. They stayed in a downstairs apartment which had also been burglarized and took our names, ages and occupations, and assured us that they would file a report for the insurance companies. They doubted that the burglars would be caught or that investigators from the Burglary Division would be interested. They recommended that we move out of the neighborhood or at least get much stronger locks.

The crime didn't make the newspapers. It hardly made a police report. It was one of 3,089,800 burglaries that year in the United States[1] (and one of three that we experienced in seven years). The burglars were never caught and our property was never recovered.

I shouldn't have been surprised. I was a lawyer, and my wife and I were living in Chicago near the church-sponsored law clinic where I had my office. We were trying to help meet the legal needs of poor people, some of them criminal defendants. So I thought I understood crime. But I had never been a victim.

Victim vs. Attorney

As a lawyer for people with little income, I was most aware of the overwhelming odds against a defendant in criminal cases. By the time charges are filed, police officers have investigated the case and have identified witnesses who can prove the prosecution's case. The prosecutor even has his own investigators to track down new leads and locate witnesses. In contrast, most indigent defendants have overworked public defenders and little else going for them.

But I believed in the system. The first case I worked on was an armed robbery case. Though the robber had worn a stocking over his head, the victim was positive that my client, who had worked for him several years earlier, was the offender. He thought he could recognize him from his size, the shape of his head and his voice. We were able to prove through hospital records and handwriting analysis that the accused had been in a hospital the night of the robbery. When the State's Attorney talked to the victim about this new evidence he admitted that he may have been wrong, and the prosecution dismissed the charges.

As a defense lawyer, I thought of victims purely as witnesses for the prosecution. What would they be asked to prove of the prosecutor's case? Could they be mistaken? A crime is a traumatic experience, particularly when it involves personal contact with the offender. The mind is not a camera able to accurately recall details. Many victims find it difficult to remember enough about the offender to make an identification.[2]

Had the victim been unfairly influenced by the police when they were looking through pictures of possible suspects? If an officer, pointing to a photograph, asks, "Was it that man?" the victim may think that the officer has inside information and may be inclined to identify the person based on that belief.[3]

Victims would often refuse to talk to me before the trial. The police or prosecutors told them that although it was my right to request an interview, defense attorneys were only trying to trip them up and it would not be wise to have anything to do with us. Of course, I disagreed. Victims were a part of the prosecution's case, and it was my job to objectively evaluate what they contributed to that case in order to prepare for the trial or plea negotiations.

But on that Monday night as I stood looking at our shattered door, I began to realize that crime is not simply an incident which begins a contest between the state and a defendant, between a prosecutor and a defense attorney. Criminal justice is not simply trial tactics, or careful preparation, or constitutional questions about the rights of defendants, or winning and losing, or even going (or not going) to prison.

Crime is first of all an encounter between a victim and an offender. It is an unexpected personal crisis in the life of one person brought on by another, and it undermines the victim's view of the world and other people. The state soon steps in and the wheels of the criminal justice system begin to turn. But crime is first an intensely personal experience with far-reaching consequences.

I spent the next day and a half repairing our door. It was slow, hard work. To repair a door jamb you have to take the entire door apart, purchase the right kind of wood, cut it to size, reinstall it, rehang the door, replace the molding and then do cosmetic repair. I am not a carpenter, but I did the work myself because we could not afford to hire one. I had to take apart the door frame and put it back together several times to get it right. I wondered if the man who kicked in our door had ever had to repair one.

Meanwhile, we spent two nights with an apartment door which would not lock. We did what we could to secure it, but we lay awake wondering whether the burglar would return.

One of the things he had taken was a new clock radio. We had bought it because our old one for some reason picked up CB broadcasts. When the music started playing the next morning and was interrupted once again by a CB transmission, I irrationally concluded that the person making the transmission was the one who had broken in. I felt violated all over again.

For a while we were preoccupied with figuring out what security measures would keep this from ever happening again. We spent a lot of time talking about what kind of locks to put in. The police had said to get better ones. In fact they told us that the kind we had simply invited burglaries. We discussed the merits of deadbolts versus metal strips to jimmyproof our current locks. We wondered if we needed a burglar alarm. Were there other self-defense steps that we should take? Yet we knew that there was no way we could guarantee our safety against someone intent on breaking in.

Meanwhile, life went on. The next morning I had to be in court, representing (ironically) a client accused of burglary. My client and two others were charged with breaking into a house at night and robbing the people in it. As they were leaving, one of the other defendants had repeatedly hit the two victims over the head with a hammer, because he was disgusted that the victims were homosexuals. Fortunately their heads had been covered with rugs to prevent them from seeing what was going on, and that protected them from serious physical injury.

The case was not up for trial that day—just for assignment to the court which would hear the case—or I might have asked to withdraw from it. Wondering what it was like to be those victims, I was not in a frame of mind to represent my client adequately.

One of the other defense attorneys had had his brand new Cadillac stolen the day before our apartment was broken into. He was very upset over that, all the more because his favorite, much-used golf clubs had been in the trunk. He had not had the car long enough to grow attached to it, and he knew that his insurance would replace it. But *those* clubs could not be replaced.

A third attorney told us how angry he had been when someone had stolen the wheel covers off his car earlier that year. It wasn't the loss that upset him as much as the fact that someone had desecrated his property. He told us he had dreamed of chasing the thief down the street with a sword.

Here we were, three people who had been victimized in relatively small ways, waiting to represent men who were charged with much more serious offenses. It did not occur to us, nor to the prosecutor or judge, that the criminal justice process we were a part of was divorced from the crimes which we and countless other victims had experienced. Technically, the defendants were not accused of robbing and beating other people. They were accused of breaking laws established by the state. The criminal justice system would not deal with the very real problem of the terrifying "relationship" that had been created between those victims and the offenders during the burglary and assault. It would only determine whether the state had enough evidence to prove beyond a reasonable doubt that our clients had committed the crimes and, if so, how they should be punished.

Victim vs. the System

Victims not only deal with offenders and their lawyers; they sometimes actually have to fight the criminal justice system itself. A New York case provides a good illustration of this. Karen Simpson was raped at knifepoint in the restroom of a public health building. A suspect was apprehended and she identified him as the man who had assaulted her.

He was seventeen years old. As a result, he could be sentenced as a youthful offender, which meant that he would receive a reduced sentence. He had been in trouble before and had a series of burglary charges pending against him in court. As a part of a plea bargain, he pleaded guilty to burglary and the rape charges were dropped. Simpson was not called as a witness. She was not even told that the prosecutor was considering the plea agreement.

She was horrified to discover that her case had been dismissed. The criminal justice system, she felt, was clearly not working in her interest. She began urging friends in the community to write to the prosecutor demanding that the charges be reinstated and that a trial be held. Eventually he bowed to the pressure, and the suspect was brought into court to again face the rape charges.

But another plea agreement was made between the prosecutor and the defense attorney. There was no trial; again, she was not consulted. The defendant pleaded guilty and was sentenced under the Youthful Offender Act.

Simpson was furious. She believed that he should have received an adult sentence. But she was even more upset that the criminal justice system was indifferent to *her* interests, the person who had been raped.[4]

If a crime is viewed as something an offender has done to a victim, then Simpson had a right to be angry. But if it is what the offender has done to the state—he has broken the law—then the prosecutor's actions were entirely appropriate. He made the decision to plea bargain because he was able to secure an easy conviction and manage a busy court docket. The victim's interests were only of secondary importance; the prosecutor's major responsibility was to obtain guilty verdicts and see that punishment was imposed.

Our country distinguishes between *criminal* and *civil* cases. The criminal courts determine whether the defendant has broken the law. The civil courts determine whether one person has injured another and, if so, how the wrongdoer will restore the victim.

If I had wanted to recover the cost of our stolen property and the damage to our apartment, I could have sued the offender in civil courts. But the job of the criminal justice system is not to recover the victim's loss. It only determines whether crimes have occurred and then how to sentence the defendants who are convicted. That is what is taught in law schools, what the criminal laws state, and what the Bar Association canon of ethics holds.

I thought I understood crime and criminal justice. But that afternoon in the shambles of our apartment, I began asking myself troubling questions.

How do we stop this kind of thing from happening? Can our formal, technical, criminal justice system really deal with personal assault like this? As a Christian, am I actually supposed to love the man who did this to us?

Those are questions I started asking myself on that cold November day. They are questions I have continued to explore during my work with Justice Fellowship. They are questions for which we must find answers.

Chapter 2

Being
Victimized

Americans are fearful. According to one study, forty per cent of us are afraid that we will become victims of violent crime. One out of four is afraid to go to familiar neighborhood places.[1]

This study distinguished between two kinds of fear. The first is "concrete fear"—a fear of specific violent crimes such as murder, rape, mugging and so forth. The second is a kind of vague uneasiness, a sense of not being safe. Examples of this "formless fear" include fear of being alone downtown, or in the neighborhood, or even at home.

We have a need to live in a safe, predictable world. Crime, particularly certain kinds of crime, threatens that safety and can become a preoccupation. People who read local newspapers filled with local crime news have a higher fear of crime than those whose papers do not give it that kind of coverage. This is particularly true if the report-ed crimes are either sensational or random.[2] And, interestingly, fear of crime is highest among those who have never experienced it.[3]

Because we are afraid of crime, we sometimes have trouble dealing with victims. They remind us of our own vulnerability, in the same way that someone with a terminal disease reminds us of our mortality. So we ignore them, we shun them, we blame them. The victim becomes invisible.

How many people do you know who have been victims of crime? We are told that twenty-seven per cent of our households are affected by crime *every year*.[4] Of course there are geographical variations, but this means on the average that one out of every four families coming to church with you on Sunday has experienced a crime in the last twelve months. A quarter of the people you work with, go to school with, or play sports with have either been victimized or live with someone who has.

But we are not aware of that. People are not proud of being vic-timized; they just don't talk about it. And if they do, we don't want to hear about it.

This is actually perpetuated by the criminal justice system. Defend-ants are charged with breaking the law; victims are at most a part of the prosecution's case. Because of the penalties facing defendants, they are provided with significant constitutional protections. Because the victims are not a party to the trial, they have none. Considerable amounts of money will be spent to punish defendants found guilty, particularly if they are sent to prison. Until recently, no money was available to compensate victims.

The Study of Victims

Around forty years ago, a new field of study emerged which early leaders called *victimology* in an attempt to separate it from *criminology*, the study of criminals.

The focus of the victimologists was to explore the ways in which the victims themselves are involved in crime. They speculated:

> In a sense, the victim shapes and molds the criminal and his
> crime. . . . The relationship between perpetrator and victim may be
> much more intricate than our criminal law, with its rough and
> mechanical definitions and distinctions, would suggest.[5]

They suggested different categories of victims based on the varying degree of *responsibility* of the victim for the crime. There was the "unrelated victim" who had no relationship with the criminal other than the crime itself. The "provocative victim's" behavior rouses the offender to commit the crime (for example, the abusing husband who is killed by his abused wife). The "precipitative victim" has done nothing to the criminal, but his behavior "instigates, tempts or allures the offender to commit a crime against the enticing victim."[6] One victimologist went so far as to call the victim and offender the "penal-couple"![7]

Many crimes occur to people who already have a relationship of some kind with the offender. The FBI reports, for example, that fifty-five per cent of all murders are committed by family members or acquaintances of the victim.[8] It may be helpful for us to know more about the dynamics of crime in such situations.

But even the existence of a prior relationship does not mean that the victim "precipitated" the offense. The overwhelming majority of victims *do not* bring it on themselves.[9] A few may, but most don't.

I suspect those early studies of victims simply reflected our tendency to blame the victim. We know that we would not "invite" a criminal attack; therefore we are reassured that crime can't happen to us. When our attention is drawn to the victims of crime, we feel vulnerable. We deal with it by concluding that they must have brought it on themselves.

Victims Respond to Crime
A look at how victims typically respond to crime will help those of us who have been victims and prepare those who may some day be

victimized (or have a loved one who is).

Each victim is unique. I was the victim of burglaries. Others have suffered through terrifying, life-threatening attacks, or have been one of hundreds or thousands who were injured through illegal business schemes.

I understood the criminal justice system. I could have taken protective measures, or I could have moved to a safer neighborhood. Many victims lack those advantages. They are confused by the court process and financially unable to protect themselves or to relocate. Perhaps this is why poor people experience more street crime than the rest of us.[10]

But we can make some generalizations about the victim experience. Several excellent books have been published in the last few years dealing with victims' responses to crime.[11] What follows is derived from these works as well as my reflections on our experience and those of other victims I have talked with.

Most victims are just like the rest of us. We all want to believe that the world is a safe place and that people can be trusted. We want to feel that we are in control of our lives and that, if things were to go out of control, we could manage the crisis. Crime undermines that. It is not an accident. Someone has done something *to us*. Suddenly we realize that we are not always able to be in control, that other people can be hostile, and that the world is often a dangerous place.

Crime creates a crisis in the lives of victims. They may have been physically injured. There are usually financial losses. There is always psychological injury, and this may affect job or academic performance, marital relationships, sexual interest or behavior. It may prompt recurring crises on special occasions, such as the birthday of a murdered loved one.

Morton Bard and Dawn Sangrey have identified three major phases in the process victims go through in dealing with crime: the Impact stage, the Recoil stage, and the Reorganization stage.[12]

The *Impact stage* is the period immediately after the crime. It is characterized by shock, denial and loneliness. In one of our other burglaries there was no sign of forced entry. We spent several weeks telling ourselves that the items must simply have been misplaced. It was not until we made a careful search through the entire apartment that we were forced to admit that someone had broken in again. The precautions we had taken after the first burglary were inadequate.

During the Impact stage, victims are confused and their defenses weakened. They are vulnerable to other people's judgments of them. A person who is helping the victim during this stage will do best to simply respond to the victim's requests even if they do not make much sense.

After our burglary, for example, I called friends who lived down the street to ask if we could come for dinner that night. I remember feeling affirmed and worthwhile when the woman I was talking to exclaimed, "Great! Please come!"—even before she knew we had been robbed. They were loving and supportive, and listened in a noncritical way when we wanted to talk. When we didn't, they talked about other things.

They and several other friends offered to let us stay with them that night, or to stay with us if we wanted the company. They did not press us when we declined.

They might have been less sensitive. They might have seen our confusion and taken over, pressing us to do things we were not inclined to do. This is the "rescue fantasy," when the helper second-guesses the victim's needs and takes charge. Although the helper is motivated by compassion, the result can actually be destructive. Crime has undermined the victim's sense of control, and a controlling friend simply reinforces this violation of personhood. "I'm so sorry, What can I do?" is a good way to start. Then do what the person asks.

It is important not to be judgmental. Pointing out ways the victims may have precipitated the crime—even agreeing with their own self-judgment—may not only undermine their self-concept, but also their trust in you. This is not a time for "clear thinking." It is a time for empathy and support.

The second stage is *Recoil.* During this period victims come to terms with the crime and begin to pull their fragmented lives together again. During Recoil, victims engage in a "recuperative rhythm," consisting of two kinds of activities: dealing with the crime and the emotions it has aroused, and then defending against them by denial. The pain is too great to deal with all at once, so victims break it into manageable pieces and buffer them with periods of denial.

That happened with me. When I went to court the next day I talked to the other attorneys about the burglary. But when our case was called, I was all business. It wasn't possible to think too much about the loss or about how much worse the crime could have been. The attorneys I talked with were helpful, both because they were sympathetic and because they did not attempt to use my emotional vulnerability to their advantage or that of their clients.

The Recoil stage is characterized by swings in mood. One day victims feel they have regained control, the next they may be dealing with raw emotion again. This is normal. Fear and anger are two common emotions and are difficult for both the victims and helpers to deal with. Fear shows itself in a variety of ways, often irrational. When I heard the CB broadcasts on our clock radio the next morning, I really believed that the person talking was the man who had broken in. We had been troubled by the interference for months, but that morning I listened closely to see whether he gave any hints about who or where he was so that I could help the police catch him. When I realized what I was doing I felt foolish. But it was a way of dealing with the other intrusion, the burglary itself.

Anger is hard to cope with because the criminal—the object of the anger—is not available.

Feelings of rage can be especially difficult because victims usually have no realistic means to vent their anger on the criminal. Most victims never see the criminal again. Even if the offender is apprehended and successfully prosecuted, the legal proceedings will take months. The absence of the criminal creates an emotional vacuum; the victim has no way to confront the person who has made him or her so angry.[13]

To counter this, victim-offender reconciliation programs have been developed in some communities which allow the victim to deal with this anger by confronting the criminal. (See chapter 12.) This is an important development, even though the encounter may take place some time after the offense.

Because anger cannot usually be expressed directly to the offender, victims find a variety of ways of dealing with it. One is through fantasy, generally about acts of revenge. Hence my attorney friend's dream of chasing his robber with a sword.

Another way is to redirect the anger at someone else. Generally this is someone close to the victim, or someone who is trying to help. It may be the landlord who should have done more to protect the building, or a family member who should not have been away when the crime occurred, or the police who should have been there to protect the victim.

Or the anger may be directed inward. Victims may attribute the crime to their own inadequate precautions. He should have locked all his windows. She should have taken a taxi instead of the bus. He should not have gone alone. Or they may view the crime as "punishment" for previous (and unrelated) bad conduct.

Helpers can respond to both kinds of redirections by acknowledging the underlying anger. This will help victims deal with the rage without becoming bogged down in an intellectual argument over whether the object of the rage is appropriate. The helper does not need to agree with the victim, just give the victim the opportunity to vent.

One of the principal questions victims are trying to resolve during the Recoil stage is why the crime happened. Identifying the cause is important because it helps victims regain a sense that life is ordered and predictable. Once again, this is an effort to come to a resolution that is emotionally as well as intellectually satisfying. Helpers need to understand the difference.

Victims often need less theology than sympathy. As Charlotte Hullinger [cofounder of Parents of Murdered Children] has pointed out, Job's Old Testament friends did well as supporters while they listened; once they began providing answers they only increased his agony. Nevertheless, victims often struggle with real faith questions and the church has an important role here.[14]

According to Howard Zehr, who has had considerable experience in this area, victims need to be reassured that the crime did not happen because God has forsaken them. Rather, in the suffering, God is present. He can transform suffering into new life, just as he raised Jesus from the dead. The resurrection which we celebrate on Easter should not mask the stark terror and pain of the crucifixion two days earlier. In Zehr's words, "The real question is not 'Why do we suffer?' but, 'What do we do with the suffering that does happen?' "[15]

We, and they, must come to understand that becoming a victim is not a sign of God's abandonment. On the contrary, God is with victims. In fact, God became a victim with us through Christ.

We, and they, must recognize that it is no sin to be a victim. It is no sin to be raped or assaulted. It is a sin, however, to commit such an act. It is also a sin to pass by on the other side of the road without responding to victims.[16]

I think that I "made sense" of our burglary in two ways. First, I personally increased the protections in our house. Although we could not afford a carpenter, I did not accept the offer of friends to help replace the door and improve the locks. It was important for me to do something myself to restore my sense of security.

Second, I wrestled with the policeman's question of why we wanted to live in that neighborhood. "There is a burglary in every block every week," he told us. I knew that was not true, but I also knew that we lived in a high-crime area. Other members of our church had also been victims of crime. One friend was raped. Two others were robbed at gunpoint, one in her own home. Several others had burglaries. We warned each other to be careful each Christmas season after several women had their purses snatched in the neighborhood. The man living in the house behind us was shot and blinded while resisting an armed robbery.

We had chosen to live in that neighborhood as a ministry. We were bringing our professional resources and the love of Christ into an economically depressed section of Chicago. But we were also gaining tremendous insight, support and love from those who lived around us. We decided to live there knowing that we might face crime. And we did. But we were there for a reason, and that reason still took priority over the risk.

The third stage in dealing with a crime is *Reorganization.* This is when the victims resolve their experiences and integrate them into their understanding of the world and themselves. The anger and rage begins to decrease, and there is emotional energy available for other experiences.

This is not a matter of "getting back to normal" as though the crime had not occurred:

> Their view of themselves and of the world will be permanently altered in some way, depending on the severity of the crime and the degree of its impact. The violation of self can hardly be called a positive experience, but it does present an opportunity for change. One of two things will happen: Either victims become reordered, reborn, put back together so that they are stronger than before, or their experiences during the crisis will promote further disorder with long-term negative consequences.[17]

Supportive people are a major factor in whether the recovery will be successful.[18]

The amount of time this can take varies, depending on the nature of the violation and the resources of the victims. These resources include previous experiences victims may have had with crises and the availability of loving, supportive friends.

Reorganization can take at least a year for rape victims or those whose loved ones have been murdered.[19] Some people never fully resolve the experience. Others are able eventually to find realistic ways to assimilate the experience into their identity and values.

The legal system may either help or hinder this resolution. How the police respond when the complaint is filed is important, because this is the first contact victims have with the apparatus which is supposed to protect them and bring wrongdoers to justice.

Unfortunately, the police are sometimes completely insensitive to the needs of victims. One midwestern couple whose adult daughter was murdered in another state were unable to find out what was happening on the investigation, apparently because the police did not consider the families of homicide victims to be "victims." Not until they contacted a victim advocacy group were they able to learn how the investigation was progressing. The organization also told them that their daughter's state had a program for financially helping the victims of violent crime and their families. The police had not thought to refer them to this compensation program.[20]

My experience—a much less serious case—was similar. The police came long after we called them and they were not interested in looking at our apartment (which I had carefully kept undisturbed so that they could look for fingerprints or do whatever they do in that kind of situation). For them it was routine. Since it seemed unlikely that they would catch the burglar, they were only interested in filing a report so that we could provide it to the insurance company.

The burglar was not, in fact, ever arrested. That is certainly typical. Out of every one hundred crimes committed, only half are reported to the police. The police respond to about thirty-seven of those, and in about ten cases they make an arrest. Of those ten arrests, only five or six will result in charges being filed. Of those, two will result in a prison sentence.[21]

We received no compensation for our losses. Because of the neighborhood we lived in and the difficulty we had had getting insurance in the first place, we were reluctant to file a claim. The deductible was high, and we were concerned that we would end up with either higher premiums or a cancelled policy. Our state did have a victim compensation program but we were not aware of it, and it was limited to victims of violent crimes.[22] Had the burglar been arrested he would most likely have been sent to prison rather than ordered to pay restitution.

In 1981, the most recent year for which this kind of information is available, victims lost $10.9 billion. Forty per cent of this—$4.1 billion—was the result of household burglaries. The median loss for each burglary was $160. ("Median" means that half the victims of burglary lost less than $160 and half lost more.)[23]

But the greatest loss is not financial. It is the loss of peace of mind. It is the sense of violation.

Most people feel their homes to be places of refuge and safety, shelters from the dangerous outside. We breathe easier behind our own familiar doors. And our homes are our nests, filled with the people and the things we love. The burglar intrudes on this security and privacy. Burglars quite literally threaten us where we live.[24]

Our burglar went through drawers, closets and file cabinets looking for money, guns or other portable property. Had he looked at our tax returns? Had he read our letters, carefully filed away? Had he touched our intimate possessions? Had he looked through our telephone directory? Had he taken down our telephone number?

He probably moved fast, knew what he was looking for, and did not bother with any of those things. But we didn't know that. Our house had been a place no one entered without an invitation. And even invited guests don't look through *everything*. He proved to us that nothing is private from someone who wants to break in. That is the kind of world we live in.

Chapter 3

Prisoners

O*n 20 July 1979,* Bradford Brown was released from Washington, D.C.'s Lorton Reformatory where he had been serving a sentence of eighteen years to life for murder. He was released because, after four years of imprisonment, he had been exonerated. The police discovered the real murderer.

The case received national publicity, and there was considerable sympathy for Brown. One year later, the District passed a compensation statute which allows people convicted unjustly to recover damages for any time they may have served as a result of their convictions. The statute was passed explicitly to give Brown and others like him compensation.

In July 1985, D.C. Superior Court Judge Ricardo M. Urbina awarded Brown $325,000 in a thirty-page opinion which outlined in detail the circumstances of his imprisonment and the effect it had on him and his family.[1]

At the time of his arrest on 11 April 1975, Bradford Brown was living with his mother and his eighteen-month-old daughter, Meiko. He and his wife had married in 1973, but separated a year later. Mr. Brown had retained custody of their daughter. He assumed her primary care—dressing her, feeding her, bathing her—and took her everywhere he went. The two were inseparable.

He was arrested at gunpoint in front of his house with his mother and daughter present. He had been identified by an eyewitness as the person who had killed a man five months earlier in an attempted robbery. He was taken to the police station for interrogation and then charged with the murder. His bond was set at $5,000. Because he was unable to raise the money, he remained in jail for seven months prior to his trial.

The jail Brown was held in has since been replaced. It was old (it had been built in the nineteenth century) and dilapidated. It was also chronically overcrowded. The first cell he was assigned to was six feet wide, eight feet long and nine feet high. He shared the cell with another inmate. It had a toilet without a seat or lid, a sink, bunkbeds and a small table and bench. It was so small only one of them could be out of bed at a time. They were locked up constantly except for meals and intermittent recreational periods. Rats, mice and roaches infested the walls. The cells were hosed out every two weeks by the authorities, sometimes with the prisoners still in them. Otherwise the prisoners were expected to do their own housekeeping.

Brown was assigned to the jail's tailor shop and moved to a different cellblock where he had his own cell and was allowed "face-to-face" visits with his mother and child. Meiko was having trouble sleeping at night because her father was gone.

Because he had no money Brown was given a court-appointed lawyer. When he told the lawyer he was innocent, the lawyer laughed.

The trial lasted five days. The eyewitness positively identified him as the murderer. His mother and other family members testified that he was with them that day at a birthday party. In his closing arguments the prosecutor called them liars, and the jury apparently agreed, finding him guilty. Two months later Brown was sentenced and transferred to Lorton Reformatory.

Lorton was also run-down and overcrowded. Health inspectors had cited the facility for its inadequate insect and rodent control, problems with its plumbing, lighting, heating and ventilation systems and overcrowding. In 1979 they rated his dormitory "substandard," noting:

The substandard conditions in the institution have serious health implications for the inmates who are required to spend extended periods of time in this closed ecological system with its overt physical, chemical and biological stresses.

These stresses may enhance the occurrence and progression of chronic and acute diseases and physical and mental disabilities.[2]

Brown's dormitory had a capacity of forty-one. While he lived there the number of inmates was usually around sixty, but once went over one hundred. The beds were placed one foot apart with a locker separating each bed. There were three toilet stalls for the dormitory, and often one or two were not working.

One night Brown was eating in the mess hall when maggots began falling from the ceiling onto a nearby table. Prison officials discovered the body of a dead cat above the ceiling.

Although there was a considerable amount of violence in the institution, Brown was never attacked. However, he witnessed bloody fights. One night he was awakened by a fight which knocked the metal locker by his bed on top of him. Two prisoners were stabbed repeatedly and fell on him. When the lights were turned on, he found that he was covered with their blood.

Another inmate was beaten with a hammer in the dark during a movie. Brown stopped going to movies.

He found that it was better not to talk about his case. He was derided when he maintained his innocence to the other prisoners. He began to deal with his growing depression by withdrawing. He worked in the tailor shop as a way of avoiding the dormitory. He volunteered for the Lorton Special Olympics Program, ran on the track, played handball and watched television.

His family remained loyal to him. Meiko, his mother, his sister and his nine-year-old son from a previous marriage visited him frequently. Eventually his son stopped coming because he could not deal with the circumstances.

Brown developed one close friend named Danny Holly. They were able to talk about his case and about what both of them were experiencing at the prison. Holly often joined him for the Sunday visits with his family. On 15 January 1978, Holly was stabbed to death.

Shortly after this Brown heard that his appeal, which had cost his family $4,500 in legal fees, had been turned down. His petition to have his sentence reduced was also denied.

A year later a police detective found that another man had done the murder, and Bradford Brown was released abruptly on 20 July 1979.

Judge Urbina, in considering what to award him, quoted from the report of a psychiatrist who until 1980 had been Chief of the Forensic Psychiatry Office for the District of Columbia:

Mr. Brown was incarcerated in Lorton Reformatory from 1975 to 1979. As I indicated in my preliminary report, the facility was a particularly bad institution during this period, and could only be described as a prison slum. There was constant stress and fear for one's physical security. Assaults and even murders were commonplace. The physical plant was in very bad shape. The dormitories were run-down and terribly overcrowded. . . . Food service and sanitation were poor. There were few really functioning rehabilitation programs and drug use was rampant. *Obviously, all of these stresses which are severe for all inmates and cause many mental breakdowns were present for Mr. Brown and greatly added to by the fact that he was incarcerated as an innocent man.*[3]

The Larger Picture

Everyone agreed that Bradford Brown should not have gone through this experience. He was innocent and should not have been punished in any way.

But what about the other men who shared his overcrowded, substandard living conditions? What about Danny Holly who was a criminal, but was also a victim of the violence that characterized the institution? The prison they were assigned to was an old facility which is still under court order for violating the Constitution's prohibition against cruel and unusual punishment.

The District of Columbia is not alone in having inhumane prisons. At the end of 1984, thirty-two states were under similar court orders to improve conditions. In eight of them the entire prison system had been ruled unconstitutional.[4]

One of the most notable things about prisons is the variety of people that are locked up in them. Charles Colson discovered this when he was incarcerated.

The prevailing public impression is that all criminals are violent. Some of them are even perceived as sub-human and innately evil, while the rest of us are innately good. The simple truth is that offenders cannot so easily be stereotyped. There is no such thing as the "typical" criminal. He just does not exist. Instead, my own experience in prison convinces me that inmates are a diverse group of individuals who represent a cross-section of society. . . .

In short, prisoners are fellow sinners and we all share with them a common heritage of sin.[5]

Just as the poor and minorities are over-represented among victims, so our prisons are disproportionately filled with them. One author wrote about this inequity in a book with a title which summarizes the problem: *The Rich Get Richer and the Poor Get Prison.*[6]

The stereotype that prisons are filled with violent, dangerous criminals turns out to be untrue. Most offenders sent to prison go for nonviolent crimes. Only 30.5 per cent of the prisoners admitted during 1983 had committed a violent crime (murder, manslaughter, rape, robbery, sexual assault and other violent offenses). This was down from 37.2 per cent in 1982.[7]

Our Response

Society tends to ignore its prisons. We prefer to make what sociologist Philip Slater calls "the toilet assumption."

> Our ideas about institutionalizing the aged, psychotic, retarded and infirm are based on a pattern of thought that we might call the Toilet Assumption—the notion that unwanted matter, unwanted difficulties, unwanted complexities and obstacles will disappear if they are removed from our immediate field of vision.[8]

This approach is both unwise and un-Christian. As we will see in the next chapter, most of the people in prison will eventually be released, and the conditions they are forced to live in is counterproductive to any hope of rehabilitation. That is the pragmatic argument for caring.

Christians have an additional motivation. We are to love our enemies as well as our neighbors. Do prison conditions meet reasonable standards of safety and health?

There were over 490,000 men and women in American prisons in mid-1985. This was more than twice as many as ten years earlier. The prison population has grown ten times faster than the general population.[9]

More people live in our prisons than live in the cities of Atlanta or Pittsburgh, in the states of Wyoming or Alaska, or in thirty-nine nations of the world.[10] Only the Soviet Union and South Africa lock up a larger percentage of their citizens than we do in the United States.[11]

There are many reasons for this high rate of imprisonment. Some of them are historical, as we will see in chapters 5 and 6. But whatever the reason, punishment and prison have become synonymous here in a way that they are not in other countries. It is in our interest to find out why, and to consider whether other approaches to punishment might not be more effective and less expensive.

Our prisons are certainly not effective. The recidivism rate (the percentage of prisoners who get into trouble again after they are released) is high. The FBI reports that 74 per cent of the people released from prison will be rearrested within four years.[12] Chief Justice Warren Burger has asked: "What business could continue with the rate of recall of its products that we see with respect to the 'products' of our prisons?"[13]

The head of the American Correctional Association put it this way: "Simply incarcerating greater numbers of offenders in the interest of protecting society, without increasing space or programs for inmates, works against the long term goal of creating a safe society."[14]

Further, locking up more people is becoming prohibitively expensive. It costs an average of $17,324 a year to keep an inmate in prison.[15] That is more than it costs to send a student to Harvard or Yale, or *three* students to a state college.[16] Building a new prison costs between $60,000 and $80,000 per cell. And over the next thirty years it will cost twelve and a half times that much to run it. In other words, a prison costing $80,000 per cell to build will cost $1 million per cell to run.[17] The total annual budget for state and federal prisons as of June 30, 1984, was *$8.5 billion!*[18]

Do we *need* to lock up all those people? Is it making us more or less safe? Is this investment worth it? These are questions increasing numbers of states have been asking in the last decade. They are coming up with some surprising answers. We will look at some of those in part IV.

But let's return to Bradford Brown and the other men and women who are serving time in prison. How can Christians respond to conditions like those Brown lived in? To answer that we need to know more about the prison experience.

Chapter 4

Being
Imprisoned

T*he Reverend* James B. Finley, chaplain of the Ohio penitentiary, wrote this in his memoirs published in 1851:

Never, no never shall we see the triumph of peace, of right, of Christianity, until the daily habits of mankind shall undergo a thorough revolution. Could we all be put on prison fare, for the space of two or three generations, the world would ultimately be the better for it. Indeed, should society change places with the prisoners, so far as habits are concerned, taking to itself the regularity, and temperance, and sobriety of a good prison, [then the goals of peace, right and Christianity would be furthered]. As it is, taking this world and the next together . . . the prisoner has the advantage.[1]

His enthusiasm helps us understand the mood of that time, only sixty years after the invention of the penitentiary. But as the experience of Bradford Brown shows us, no sane person today would suggest that we improve the quality and moral character of life by putting innocent (or even guilty) people in today's prison environments.

I have never served time in a prison, so I cannot speak from personal experience. But I have visited prisons, and I have spent time with people who are currently in prison or who have previously "done time." This has convinced me, as it has everyone who has been closely connected with prisons in any way, that although we may need to have them, they are seldom beneficial environments for the people who must live in them. We should avoid sending people there unless we have no alternative.

We can make some generalizations about life in prison. Almost thirty years ago, sociologist Gresham M. Sykes noted five common traits of prison experience: the deprivation of liberty, the deprivation of goods and services, the deprivation of heterosexual relationships, the deprivation of autonomy, and the deprivation of security.[2] Let us look at each of these to understand something of the prison experience.

Loss of Liberty

The loss of liberty is what imprisonment is supposed to be. We take away the offender's freedom to live among us.

But we need to be reminded from time to time that this is a real loss. I received a letter from an irate man several years ago complaining about a new jail opening in his county. He noted that it was air conditioned and equipped with television sets. *"But for the loss of freedom,"* he wrote, "it sounds like a vacation." His comments reminded me of a famous statement by George Bernard Shaw:

> What sane man, I ask the clamorers, would accept an offer of free board, lodging, clothing, waiters in attendance at a touch of the bell, medical treatment, spiritual advice, scientific ventilation and sanitation, technical instruction, liberal education, and the use of

a carefully selected library, with regular exercise daily and sacred music at frequent intervals, even at the very best of the Ritz Hotels, if the conditions were that he should never leave the hotel, never speak, never sing, never laugh, never see a newspaper, and write only one sternly censored letter and have one miserable interview at long intervals through the bars of a cage under the eye of a warder?[3]

While conditions have changed, the question remains a good one. Who would request one, two, five or twenty-five years at a Holiday Inn, eating catered food, on condition that they never leave the room? And as courts in thirty-two states have ruled, our prisons do not come close to the quality of Holiday Inn motels—they do not even meet minimal health and safety standards.[4]

When I was in fifth grade, as part of a history course, four of us debated whether slavery had been a good thing for Black people. I had the easier side, arguing that it had not. I wondered what the other side would come up with as a plausible argument for slavery. Their main point turned out to be that prior to being brought to the United States, slaves did not have Western food, medical treatment or Christianity.

We won the debate easily. But years later I was shocked to discover that those had been the very arguments advanced by slave owners to oppose abolition. Apparently freedom was not too high a price to pay for those other advantages, at least in the view of those who stood to lose if the institution of slavery were abolished.

We can sometimes see more clearly after the fact. Freedom was the central issue in slavery, not simply one of the factors that should be balanced with others. The loss of freedom for those who are incarcerated is the basic deprivation and is by itself sufficient punishment. The loss of freedom for an innocent person is grounds for substantial civil damages in the District of Columbia, as Bradford Brown found out.

Prisoners lose more than the right to move where they please. They

are cut off from family and friends, work and church, not because
they want peace and quiet, but because they have been found guilty
of a crime.

Bradford Brown was fortunate to be in a prison near his family and
to have a mother and daughter who maintained contact with him.
(Most inmates receive no visits and no mail.) Yet even with those
advantages, we saw the strains that resulted from his being locked up.
His daughter could not sleep because he was not home. His son had
to stop coming because he could not cope with seeing his father
under those conditions. This is not unusual. The incarceration of
their parents affects children in a variety of ways. Blind ratings for
various social and psychological characteristics were given by teachers
to children of incarcerated fathers and to children in control groups.
The children of incarcerated fathers were more frequently rated be-
low average. Declining academic performance soon followed imprisonment of the father.[5]

Loss of freedom is a perpetual reminder that the prisoner has been
judged and convicted. I am amazed at the lack of self-worth in the
prisoners that I meet. Many of them were successful before they were
charged and convicted. Some are doing time in relatively decent prisons. Yet their self-esteem has slipped so low that they cannot believe
anyone could care about them at all.

Their self-concept has been destroyed by the experience of trial,
conviction and sentencing. Friends are now busy and unavailable.
Children carry a stigma. Prospective employers are uninterested in
someone with a record. Even some churches ask that they not attend
for fear that they will "pollute" the young people.

Some have suggested that inmates do not care. They are unconcerned about what society values, and its condemnation is unimpor-
tant to them. But this is not true of most prisoners.

For the great majority of criminals in prison . . . the evidence suggests that neither alienation from the ranks of the law-abiding nor
involvement in a system of criminal value is sufficient to eliminate

the threat to the prisoner's ego posed by society's rejection. . . . The prisoner is never allowed to forget that, by committing a crime, he has foregone his claim to the status of a full-fledged, *trusted* member of society.[6]

Prison Fellowship conducts two-week work projects using furloughed inmates to rehabilitate run-down houses. The inmates live with Christian families and spend their days painting, plastering, doing carpentry, installing insulation or roofing, and whatever else needs to be done. Time after time the response of the inmates is gratitude—they have been given a tangible way to pay their debt to society rather than simply vegetate in a prison cell. They are grateful for the freedom to serve someone who is in more desperate straits than they, even though that freedom is so closely structured that they have no control over how they spend their time.

Loss of Goods and Services
The loss of goods and services is felt in at least two ways. First is the absence of personal property that has particular significance to the prisoner. As we discussed earlier, our material possessions are extensions of ourselves. These are taken from prisoners. Charles Colson writes of his experience:

Bleven started through each piece of clothing and every personal article I had carried with me. "This goes, this goes—this—this," he said, listing items which were to be shipped home.

"No," he said after deliberating a moment with himself about a pair of my shorts. "You can't bring these in, you can wear them only if you can't find a pair around here." The list was now two pages long. Next came my wallet, all personal identification, pictures of Patty and the kids. How I hated to part with my identification! "All jewelry must be removed," Bleven said almost apologetically now, looking at my class ring.

"I wear it as a wedding ring and I'm not sure I can get it off," I protested. Patty had given it to me.

"Sorry. Regulations. I'll have to have it."[7]

There might be a symmetry in punishing burglars and thieves by taking away all their personal possessions. It could be argued that this would give them a feel for the loss their victims experienced. But this is not the reason that prisoners lose their personal effects. It is for purposes of convenience, control and—prisoners would add—humiliation.

The second way goods and services are lost is that often basic material needs are not met. Bradford Brown slept in his clothing during the winter because there was not enough heat. I have seen a memorandum from the supply officer of a major midwestern prison stating that due to overcrowding there were not enough shoes to go around. Prisoners were walking barefoot.

In most of the thirty-two states under court order because of prison conditions, the courts have identified inadequate living conditions or medical treatment as a major reason for finding the prison system unconstitutional. One judge noted that a prison was holding hundreds of prisoners for as much as twenty-three hours per day in less space than was required for dogs and cats in a nearby city.[8]

Loss of Heterosexual Relationships

Because of sexual segregation in prison, inmates lose the opportunity for heterosexual contact. They live in an environment which does not offer the balance that comes from having both men and women around. As Sykes noted at the maximum security facility for men in New Jersey,

in addition to these problems stemming from sexual frustration per se, the deprivation of heterosexual relationships carries with it another threat to the prisoner's image of himself—more diffuse, perhaps, and more difficult to state precisely and yet no less disturbing. The inmate is shut off from the world of women which by its very polarity gives the male world much of its meaning. Like most men, the inmate must search for his identity not simply within himself but also in the picture of himself which he finds reflected in the eyes of others; and since a significant half of his audience is denied him, the inmate's self-image is in danger of becoming half complete, fractured, a monochrome without the hues of reality.[9]

Prisoners who enjoyed a meaningful family relationship before going into prison often find that relationship strained beyond its limits because of the forced separation. Most prisons are located long distances from major population areas, which makes visiting difficult. The spouse outside of prison has increased responsibilities for working as well as caring for the rest of the family; this further restricts the opportunities for coming to the prison. Wives of male prisoners face the additional problems of stigmatization, financial and housing difficulties, loneliness and sexual frustration.[10] It should not surprise us, then, to discover that many marriages do not survive imprisonment. One prisoner, locked up for the first time, described the cost to his family:

☐ A wife I love very much hurts every time she sees me or even thinks of me, so she does neither and is divorcing me.

☐ My 14-year-old daughter took an overdose of sleeping pills the week before Christmas.

☐ My 16-year-old son is terribly confused. He has no father to speak with and only the miserable example of an admitted thief to look to during the most important years of his life.

☐ My father is dying in a hospital in another state and will go without hearing me say "Goodbye, I love you," or having me hold his hand.[11]

Loss of Autonomy

The inmate's life is regulated to the point that his ability and need to make decisions is all but eliminated. Standard clothing is provided. Food is served at specified hours and the inmates eat what is given them. Work, if it is available, is assigned, as are educational opportunities. Hours are determined by regulation. Visitation is done at specified intervals.

The stated justification for these regulations is security. In order to manage a large population and to control contraband, the administration must be able to control the life of the inmate population, even in areas that seem trivial.

Courts have ruled on some such regulations over the last twenty years and balanced them against security concerns. Beginning with religious freedom cases in the late 1960s, courts have often held that, due to institutional over-regulation, inmates have been deprived of constitutional rights to worship, to bring grievances to court, to communicate with attorneys and the media, to receive medical care, and to express political views.[12] Recently, however, in cases where there are not clear violations of the Constitution, the courts are again deferring to the administrations, stating that it is not possible or wise for the judiciary to impose its views on those who are responsible (and presumably trained) for running the prisons.

But even with the new freedoms and in an ideally run, constitutional prison, autonomy is limited. This is perhaps most apparent in the adjustment that a newly released prisoner must make in returning to free society. John Irwin, himself an ex-prisoner, describes this as "taking care of business":

> The ability to schedule one's time is lost in the slow-paced, routinized prison life. The convict is accustomed to having his life regulated by an assortment of bells, horns, whistles, and commands. Once outside he must relearn to parcel out his day for himself, but this is a skill that has many obscure contours and requires unnoticed resources (for instance an alarm clock) and a period of practice.[13]

Another dimension of this loss of autonomy is the lack of privacy. The need for institutional control is met only if the prisoner is visible at all times. Bradford Brown's dormitory had unscreened toilets and urinals along one wall. From time to time the inmates were allowed to suspend sheets in front of the toilets to achieve a modicum of privacy. Because assaults frequently occur in showers, correctional officials supervise these areas. In some states equal protection employment laws have resulted in female guards supervising male shower facilities and vice versa.

Loss of Security

Some prisoners are locked up because they are dangerous. These violent offenders are placed with others who are not violent, but who must learn to live with them for substantial periods of time. Judge Urbina, in awarding damages to Bradford Brown, noted this problem.

> Violence was widespread in the Central Facility when Plaintiff was there. Assaults, both inmate-on-inmate and inmate-on-guard, were commonplace. Many resulted in serious injuries, a few in deaths. Weapons of all types, some homemade and some smuggled into the facility as contraband, were prevalent. They included knives, hatchets, pipes, "shanks" and handguns.
>
> Furthermore, roving bands of homosexuals known among the inmates as "wolfpacks" preyed on other inmates, to the extent of occasionally pulling new arrivals off the incoming bus, taking them to a dormitory and assaulting them. Some of the violence was gratuitous and apparently without motive. Assaults occurred which were never officially reported.[14]

The chances of being murdered in prison are much higher than outside.[15] It takes little imagination to understand the effects this kind of environment can have on prisoners. Inmates realize that at some point they may be tested. How they respond determines the treatment they will receive for the rest of their stay. One former prisoner explained it to me this way: "I knew that I would have to fight and that if I stood up the first time I would be all right after that."

Certainly not every prisoner is assaulted. But the pressure of living in this kind of environment takes its toll. In the opinion of Dr. William Perdue, former head psychologist at the Virginia State Penitentiary, the pressures of prison life coupled with the fear of inmate assaults drive scores of prisoners to mental hospitals. Often commitment to an institution is accompanied by a change in the prisoner's personality. Some become more defensive and wary of potential assailants. Others who have been passive become more aggressive.[16]

All of this has been greatly exacerbated by overcrowding since Sykes published his study on deprivation. Now, at least two-thirds of all prisoners live in overcrowded facilities[17] due to the tremendous growth of our prison population since 1975.

Everyone, from governors to law enforcement officials, cites overcrowding as the primary problem facing the criminal justice system today. Some have estimated that more than $10 billion in construction is needed to create sufficient space for all these prisoners.

Studies have amply documented what common sense would tell us: overcrowding produces tremendous strains on prisoners and correctional officials alike. Illnesses rise, death and suicide rates increase, and discipline declines.[18] Violence and other misconduct increase as prisons become overcrowded.[19]

But overcrowding may harm the general public as well. Prisoners graduating from these kinds of facilities are less capable of adjusting to life outside. And some dangerous offenders may not be going to prison in the first place because of the overcrowding. The Attorney General's Task Force on Violent Crime found that a substantial number of defendants who should be incarcerated receive probation instead because judges know there is no room for them in prison.[20]

One response to overcrowding is to build more prisons. But it is increasingly apparent that public officials cannot build their way out of this crisis—it is just too expensive. California is building $1.2 billion worth of new prisons. But when those 17,000 beds have been completed in 1987, the Department of Corrections estimates that it will still be 8,000 to 9,000 beds short.[21]

Other states have begun to explore a range of alternatives for dealing with the overcrowding crisis. Some new construction may be necessary. But as officials have analyzed their prison populations, they have realized that the public could be protected without incarcerating some kinds of criminals. These states have developed programs to divert those nondangerous offenders into other forms of punishment. We will look at some of those in chapter 12.

The extent to which prisoners feel that they themselves are victims is remarkable. They believe that the criminal justice system did not work for them the way it is supposed to, that the things they experience in prison are far worse than they deserve for breaking the law. And most of all, they are acutely aware that the punishment they are being given has nothing to do with the crime they committed. *They know that being in prison does not address the harm caused their victims.*

Their prison experience is not forcing them to accept responsibility for what they have done. Instead, it is motivating them to fight the system that they believe is treating them unjustly. Chief Justice Warren Burger has described it this way:

> So we see a paradox, even while we struggle toward correction, education and rehabilitation of the offender, our system encourages prisoners to continue warfare with society. The result is that whatever may have been the defendant's hositility toward the police, the witnesses, the prosecutors, the judge and jurors, and the public defender who failed to win his case, those hostilities are kept alive. How much chance do you think there is of changing or rehabilitating a person who is encouraged to keep up years of constant warfare with society?[22]

The Chief Justice's solution is to limit access of inmates to the courts in order to impose finality on the legal procedures. But I wonder if that will really resolve the problem. If the hostility is there, cutting off one avenue for its expression will simply cause it to build up and be vented somewhere else.

Another way to approach the problem would be to recognize that the criminal justice system does not currently require the offender to accept responsibility for the injury caused to the victim. Just as victims are hurt by the inability to meet with offenders to vent anger and try to understand why they did what they did, so offenders are hurt by never being held accountable to the victims. Our criminal justice system separates the two, devalues them, and treats crime as an injury to the state. As we have seen, this is not satisfying to victims. It also helps explain why the prison experience is not the rehabilitative process we want it to be or the kind of punishment, particularly for nonviolent offenders, that serves society's long-term interests.

Conclusion

We have looked at two snapshots. One is of a burglary victim standing next to victims of other crimes, some more terrible, some less severe. In the background stands a fearful community not sure how to respond.

The other is of a prisoner, surrounded by other offenders, some serving shorter sentences, others awaiting execution. Behind them, at a great distance, stands the same community, just as fearful and uncertain as in the first picture, but also angry.

Victims and prisoners are not the only people affected by crime. But I have picked these two groups because they show clearly that something is terribly wrong in our justice system.

For one brief moment the victim and the offender confront each other. The crime establishes a relationship in which one wounds another. But we never deal with the wound. We try offenders when we catch them. And we sometimes send them to prison, not for the injury done to the victims, but because they broke the law. So now we have two wounds, and no healing.

The wounds multiply. Friends and neighbors of the victim, concerned for their own safety, start taking greater precautions. Fear is also a wound. The families of prisoners, unable to deal with the separation and stigma, begin to draw apart. Another wound. The victims who are reorganizing and the prisoners who are being released discover that the community cannot accept them as victims or ex-prisoners, and they conceal that part of themselves. More wounds.

We must hold offenders accountable. They have broken the law; they have hurt others. If we do not insist that those who commit crimes be held responsible for their actions, we begin a slide into anarchy. But the offender can be held responsible in many ways. It is in our best interest to find those ways that heal wounds, not create new ones.

Before we explore why this is important, and how it could be done, we need to understand how we got here. Why do we treat crimes this way? What is the rationale for this approach?

Part II

How We Got Here

Chapter 5

The Rise of State-Centered Justice

T*he two men met* at the river where each had come to fish. Each had a grievance with the other, a feud that had been simmering for weeks.

Perhaps that is why, when their lines tangled, angry words were exchanged. Words changed to blows. And then one stooped down, picked up a rock and clubbed the other on the head.

The injured man did not die, but he required extensive medical care and a long recuperation. Eventually he was able to move around, supported by a cane.

This was not a case of self-defense. The offender had not been in fear of losing his life; he had been angry. What should we do with him?

In most states he would be charged with serious felonies: assault with a deadly weapon and probably attempted murder. If convicted he would serve a substantial prison sentence.

Let us assume that this had happened four thousand years ago, in Old Testament times. How would the offender be punished?

> If men quarrel and one hits the other with a stone or with his fist and he does not die but is confined to bed, the one who struck the blow will not be held responsible [i.e., be executed for murder] if the other gets up and walks around outside with his staff; however, he must pay the injured man for the loss of his time and see that he is completely healed. (Ex 21:18-19)

In other words, the offender would not be executed or go to jail. But he would be obligated to pay for the medical treatment and lost wages of the victim.

The Focus of Ancient Law: The Victim

It is surprising to most people that early legal systems which form the foundation of Western law emphasized the need for offenders and their families to settle with victims and their families. The offense was considered principally a violation against the victim and the victim's family.[1] While the common welfare had been breached, and the community therefore had an interest and responsibility in seeing that the wrong was addressed and the offender punished, the offense was not considered primarily a crime against the state as it is today.

☐ Old Testament law emphasized that the victim be repaid through restitution (see chapter 10).

☐ The Code of Hammurabi (around 1700 B.C.), a collection of Babylonian laws, provided for restitution in the case of property crimes.[2]

☐ The Code of Ur-Nammu, a Sumerian king (around 2050 B.C.), included provisions for restitution even in the case of violent offenses.[3]

☐ In the Code of Lipit-Ishtar (around 1875 B.C.), the king of Isin required restitution when a householder neglected to maintain his property and as a result someone was able to break into the house of a neighbor. He was required to compensate the neighbor for his losses.[4]

☐ The Code of Eshnunna (around 1700 B.C.), a Mesopotamian kingdom, provided for specific compensation when the victim lost his nose, his eye, his ear, or a tooth.[5]

☐ In the ninth book of *The Iliad,* Homer (around the ninth century B.C.) refers to the practice of victim restitution. Ajax challenges Achilles for not accepting compensation offered by Agamemnon, noting that even the murderer of a brother may, by paying compensation, remain free among his own family.

☐ Roman law also required compensation of the victim. According to the Law of the Twelve Tables (449 B.C.), convicted thieves had to pay double the value of the stolen goods. If the property was discovered hidden in the thief's house, he had to pay three times its value. If he had resisted the house search, or if he had stolen the object using force, he had to pay four times its value.[6]

☐ The Roman historian Tacitus (roughly A.D. 55 to A.D. 117) wrote that among ancient Germanic tribes even murder was punished by paying a fine of cattle and sheep, and that this satisfied the family of the murder victim, since ongoing feuds were destructive of the community.[7]

☐ The earliest surviving collection of Germanic tribal laws is the *Lex Salica,* promulgated by King Clovis soon after his conversion to Christianity in A.D. 496. It includes restitutionary sanctions for offenses ranging from homicides to assaults to theft.[8]

☐ Anglo-Saxon law developed elaborate systems of compensation. Around A.D. 600, Ethelbert, ruler of Kent, issued the Laws of Ethelbert. They contain remarkably detailed restitution schedules, differentiating, for example, the value of the four front teeth from those next to them, and those teeth from all the rest. Each finger (and its fingernail) had a specified value.[9]

In each of these diverse cultures the response to what we now call "crime" was to hold offenders and their families accountable to victims and their families. Crime was understood to be an event involving the parties, as well as their kin, in the context of the community.[10] This reflected a basic understanding that a relationship existed between victims and offenders, and that this relationship needed to be addressed in responding to the wrong. Victims were a key part of the process for pragmatic reasons (they and their families insisted on this), but also for reasons of simple justice—no adequate response to the crime could exclude the victim.

The Focus Changes

The Norman Conquest of Europe marked the beginning of the end of this approach. When William the Conqueror became king of England, he took title to all land. He then portioned it out to his supporters and to the church.[11] He and his descendants asserted increasing control over the process by which crimes and other judicial matters were disposed of.

But where earlier developments were designed to keep family feuds from tearing apart the community,[12] King William and his descendants were struggling for control of the legal process for the sake of political power. They were replacing local systems of dispute resolution (established by the barons) and were competing with the growing influence of the church over secular matters. The church had issued the Canon Law, which comprehensively regulated every dimension of life. The secular authorities responded to this by creating similar law codes.[13]

A mechanism which the English kings successfully used in this struggle for control was the "king's peace." King Henry I, the son of William the Conqueror, issued the *Leges Henrici* in 1116. These laws established thirty judicial districts throughout the country and gave them jurisdiction over "certain offenses *against the king's peace,* arson, robbery, murder, false coinage, and crimes of violence."[14]

Anything which jeopardized this peace became a subject of the king's jurisdiction. This gave the king control over criminal cases as breaches of that peace. Criminal punishments were no longer viewed primarily as ways of restoring the victims of crime, but instead as means of redressing the "injury" to the king.

The king not only gained power, he also enriched his treasury. Because of the existing emphasis on compensating victims, the early codes required restitution but confiscated some of the payments for the king's treasury. Over time, the amount confiscated from the victim increased, and eventually restitution was seldom ordered—the defendant was simply fined.[15]

Furthermore, feudal custom held that when a vassal "broke faith" with his ruler, his possessions reverted to the lord—this was called *escheat*.

The Norman word for such a breach of faith was "felony." In England after the Norman Conquest the most serious crimes came to be called felonies because they were considered to be breaches of the fealty owed by all people to the king as guardian of the realm. (The felon's land escheated to his lord, however, and only his chattels to the crown.)[16]

As a result, *the victim had no remedy*. The criminal proceeding generated fines for the king. In felony cases, conviction meant that *all* the offender's property reverted to his lord and to the king. The victim would have no way to recover through civil action against the impoverished offender.

The punishment of crime had become the province of the state. Recovery by the victim was a private matter to be settled in the civil courts. The state's interest in criminal cases was in fixing the responsibility of the offenders and punishing them, not restoring the victims. The role of victims was only to help establish that a wrong had been done.[17]

The "golden age of the victim"[18]—the period when the system of justice emphasized compensation to the victim—had ended. It was replaced with what could be called the "golden age of the state," which continues today. Now the *criminal* justice system emphasizes controlling the injury to the state through various forms of punishment designed to deter, incapacitate or reform criminals. If victims want to recover their losses, they must sue in civil courts.

Chapter 6

People vs. Defendant

S*hortly after I began* practicing law, Valerie Crandall came to see me. She had been assaulted and harrassed by a former employer, Mark Jones. He was convinced that she had engineered his termination so that she could take his job. He had actually been fired for incompetence, and she did not want his position. She was filling it until the agency's Board found a permanent replacement.

Valerie had received threatening calls at her home and the office, and she finally called the police after two of Jones's friends threatened to kill her if she did not stop coming to work.

The police were very helpful. She filed charges against Jones and then asked me to represent her in the criminal proceedings. I explained to her that she did not need a lawyer. Prosecutors would be assigned to the case, and they would give her the assistance she needed.

But she had already called the prosecutors, and they were too busy to talk with her. In the meantime, she continued to receive threatening calls.

Jones had hired a skilled attorney who was preparing him for the trial. When I spoke with the attorney, I learned that he had already discussed with the prosecutors a plea bargain to dismiss the charges with both Valerie and Jones agreeing not to contact each other. The prosecutors were inclined to accept that agreement but had not discussed it with her. They were waiting for the trial date.

Valerie was very concerned. It was clear to her that the prosecutors were not "her" lawyers, and she understood that they had many cases to clear as quickly as possible. But she had never called Jones, and she was unhappy with a settlement that not only implied she was at fault, but which gave her no protection. Because of my calls and the support of the police, the prosecutors finally obtained a court order prohibiting Jones from having any contact with her.

Valerie was confused about why her interests seemed to be so different from the prosecutors. But, as we have seen, the reasons are historical and political. The criminal code viewed Jones's actions as an injury to the state, not to Valerie.

Our legal system defines crime as lawbreaking, an offense against law and government. Therefore, it is the government that responds, with primary emphasis upon the law and the offender.

This approach not only leaves the victim out but hides the real meaning of crime. Crimes of violence and of property are fundamentally offenses against individuals. They are violations of the self, of who we are and of our private space. This is true for property crimes as well as violent crimes because property is in many ways an extension of the self.[1]

But victims are not the only ones who have been affected by this redefinition of crime. There are profound implications for offenders as well, stemming from three developments: the creation of protections for the defendant against the state, the rise of schools of criminology, and the development of a new form of punishment.

Protecting the Accused

Out of the struggle between the kings of England and the nobility came a series of protections for those accused of crimes. These protections were eventually incorporated into the United States Constitution in the Bill of Rights. We must remember that these are an expression not of leniency on the part of the framers of the Constitution, but of an appreciation, gained from experience, of the need to control the powers of the state in criminal matters.

The struggle between the kings and the barons for political control lasted for centuries. During this time, the kings made use of all their powers to assert their authority. But on several notable occasions, the nobility forced concessions from the king. One of the most famous is the Magna Carta, which King John was forced to sign in 1215. One of the clauses of this document reads: "No free man shall be taken or imprisoned or dispossessed, or outlawed, or banished, or in any way destroyed . . . except by the legal judgment of his peers or by the law of the land."[2]

Centuries later, Henry VII created a new court. It was called the Star Chamber after the room in the palace where it conducted its proceedings. It was used to suppress rebellious barons and its proceedings were characterized by secrecy, confessions obtained through torture, and the absence of jury trials. Its judgments were arbitrary and often extremely severe. It was used from the fifteenth century to 1641 when Charles I abolished it.[3]

As a result of the Star Chamber and other abuses of the kings' powers, Parliament passed the Habeas Corpus Act in 1679 and compelled William and Mary to accept the Bill of Rights as a condition of their receiving the throne of England in 1688. The Habeas Corpus Act made it possible for anyone who believed he was unjustly imprisoned to require the government to explain in open court the reasons for his detention. The Bill of Rights, among other things, prohibited excessive fines and bail, as well as cruel punishment.[4]

These protections were needed because of the growing power of the state. As the state became stronger, individuals needed protection. The process which had led to the king asserting exclusive jurisdiction over criminal cases led to the guarantees of individual freedom and protection which are contained in the Constitution.

The Study of Criminology

Criminology is the scientific study of crime, criminals and the methods available to the state to reduce crime and punish those who break the law. It developed only after the state had assumed jurisdiction over criminal behavior, and it has had a tremendous impact on criminal justice.[5] Let's look briefly at the two major schools of criminology, focusing both on their definitions of crime and their understanding of what causes (and therefore what might prevent) violations of the law.

The *classical school* of criminology centered around the late-eighteenth-century writings of Cesare Beccaria in Italy (1738-1794) and Jeremy Bentham in England (1748-1832).[6] Reacting to the severity of contemporary punishments and the arbitrary use of state powers to penalize human behavior, the classicists emphasized free will, rationalism and utilitarianism.[7]

The classicists insisted that the state strictly define what was to be considered criminal behavior and that it establish a legal framework for the administration of criminal justice. One of their greatest contributions to criminal law was the principle *nulla poena sine lege:* there was to be no punishment without law.[8]

They believed that people are rational beings with the freedom to choose to live a law-abiding life. This choice was based on the pleasure/pain principle. To deter the criminal, then, it was necessary that a sufficient amount of punishment be imposed quickly and surely to offset the prospective benefits of criminal activity.[9] Too much punishment, however, was counterproductive:

> The severity of punishment itself emboldens men to commit the very wrongs it is supposed to prevent. . . . The countries and times most notorious for severity of penalties have always been those in which the bloodiest and most inhumane of deeds were committed.[10]

This was because it might encourage criminals to commit additional crimes in order to avoid punishment for a single one, and because it made convictions difficult to obtain from juries who were aware of the likely punishment.

Beccaria argued that "the certainty of a punishment, even if it be moderate, will always make a stronger impression than the fear of another which is more terrible but combined with the hope of impunity."[11]

Later writers, in what has been called the neoclassical school, modified the notion of free will by introducing notions of limited responsibility, extenuating circumstances, premeditation and by recognizing that children, the mentally defective or insane should be excused from responsibility.[12]

In the late nineteenth century a major challenge to the classical school arose. The *positivist school* centered around the writings of Cesare Lombroso (1836-1909), Enrico Ferri (1856-1928) and Raffaele Garofalo (1852-1934). The positivists viewed crime as a determined phenomenon, not as a utilitarian decision to violate the law. Where the classicists emphasized the development of a legal framework, the positivists were sociologists, preoccupied with discovering the causes of crime. They borrowed from the methodology of the natural sciences and examined offenders and their surroundings.[13]

Lombroso believed that there were biological explanations for crime. He later modified his views to include environmental factors as well. He is well known for his contention that there was a criminal physiology. In his earlier works he stated that a criminal was an evolutionary throwback who could be identified by an assymetrical face, defects and peculiarities of eyes, large ears, unusually long arms and so on. This notion has been demonstrated to be false, of course, and Lombroso retreated from some of his stronger generalizations in his later works.[14] A much more sophisticated argument for a constitutional contribution to criminal behavior has recently been advanced by two Harvard professors, James Q. Wilson and Richard J. Herrnstein.[15]

Ferri argued that social, economic and political, as well as biological, factors were involved in criminal behavior. Garofalo worked to develop a definition of "natural" crime, which identified that behavior which no culture could fail to recognize as criminal and therefore punish.[16]

These early attempts at explaining why people commit crimes may seem crude now. But the influence of the positivists cannot be overstated. The search for the causes of crime and approaches the state can take to reform individual offenders has been a major characteristic of American criminology.[17] As a result, most of our efforts have sought to discover what form of punishment would most likely keep offenders from committing crimes.

The Development of the Penitentiary
The unique American contribution to the punishment of criminals has been the prison. The use beginning in 1790 of the Walnut Street Jail in Philadelphia for punishing convicted criminals was an historic event.[18]

1. Early experiments. There had been a few instances where imprisonment was used as punishment before 1790. Monasteries in Europe in the Middle Ages had used imprisonment as a form of discipline. Initially, these were more retreats than prisons, but Jean Mabillon, a seventeenth-century monk wrote that eventually "a frightful kind of prison, where daylight never entered, was invented, and since it was designed for those who should finish their lives in it, received the name 'vade in Pace' ['go in peace']."[19]

Perhaps influenced by the monastic prisons, Pope Clement XI founded St. Michele in Rome in 1704, a prison for habitual juvenile delinquents. In 1682, William Penn, the Governor of Pennsylvania, initiated a law which made hard labor in a house of correction the principal punishment for most crimes. (This law was subsequently repealed.) Hippolyte Vilain XIII built a house of correction in Belgium in the early 1770s.[20]

But these were isolated experiments in using incarceration as punishment. Aside from these, prisons before 1790 were either places of detention before trial or punishment, places to hold insolvent debtors until their creditors were satisfied, or places to confine prisoners of war. The prisons referred to in Scripture (as we shall see in chapter 10) were used for this purpose.[21]

And how were seventeenth- and eighteenth-century criminals punished? Property offenders were usually required to pay fines and restitution to the victim. Others were subjected to a wide variety of corporal punishments, ranging from whipping (the most commonly used) to stocks, the pillary, branding and the dunking stool (in which village gossips were strapped and plunged into a nearby pond or stream). If these financial or corporal punishments did not discourage the offender from committing new crimes, the sentence was either banishment or execution by hanging.[22]

It is important to note—because this is so different from contemporary practice—that these sentences were almost always carried out in public, with the dual intention of humiliating the offender and deterring potential criminals.[23]

2. *Isolation and reflection: the "penitentiary" approach.* The Quakers, who were the driving force behind the Walnut Street Jail, believed that crime was caused by the criminal's environment.[24] Removing offenders from that environment and placing them in isolation with a Bible and regular visits from the warden and a minister would encourage them to reflect on their guilt and repent. So the name they gave their institution was *penitentiary.*[25]

The prisoners were kept in small cells, six feet wide, eight feet long and nine feet high. Each cell had a small yard attached to it. They had no contact with other prisoners or with their families. There was no recreation; the food was spare. They heard sermons regularly.

The experiment failed. Plagued by escapes, riots and financial problems, the prison closed in 1835. But by then, Pennsylvania had built two new, large penitentiaries: Western Penitentiary near Pittsburgh, and Eastern Penitentiary in Philadelphia.

Charles Dickens, after a visit to the Eastern Penitentiary, wrote:

> Over the head and face of every prisoner who comes into this melancholy house, a black hood is drawn; and in this dark shroud, an emblem of the curtain between him and the living world, he is led to the cell from which he never again comes forth, until his whole term of imprisonment has expired. He never hears of wife and children; home or friends; the life or death of any single creature. He sees the prison officers, but with that exception he never looks upon a human countenance, or hears a human voice. He is a man buried alive; to be dug out in the slow round of years; and in the meantime dead to everything but torturing anxieties and horrible despair.[26]

According to Thomas Mott Osborne, a leading prison official at the beginning of this century, the Quakers "showed a touching faith in human nature, although precious little knowledge of it."[27]

3. Discipline and hard work: the "Auburn" approach. By 1825, the New York prison system had become the chief rival to the Pennsylvania system. The enthusiasm of the Quakers, despite the failure of their initial experiment, was contagious, and a number of states began experimenting with imprisonment of convicts. For a while, it was simply the idea of incarceration that captured the imaginations of state legislatures. Connecticut, for example, used an abandoned copper mine as its prison. "Prisoners served their sentences in slime-covered caverns with water dripping from the ceilings."[28]

New York, too, began imprisoning convicts. Its first facility, Newgate, was modeled after the Walnut Street Jail and was built in the late 1790s. In 1802 it was torn by a violent riot and mass escape that was halted only through the use of military force. This led Thomas Eddy, the New York pioneer of prisons, to conclude that the architecture was wrong. He proposed that inmates be held in solitary cells at night, but be brought together during the day to work in total silence. Isolation from negative environmental influences could be preserved through silence and regimen, but the discipline of work would not only instill improved habits but also help defray the cost of the prison.[29]

Auburn, New York, was the site of the first prison built along these lines, and this approach became known as the Auburn system. For the next several decades it vied with the Pennsylvania system as other states and countries decided what kind of prison they would develop. The Auburn system emerged victorious thanks in part to aggressive support from reformers committed to its philosophy.

While the Pennsylvania system operated under the assumption that what prisoners needed was the time and isolation to reflect on their sins in order to reform, the Auburn system was more direct. "In order to reform a criminal you must first break his spirit," said Elam Lynds, warden of Sing Sing prison in New York. The purpose of prison was to dominate offenders, break them and return them to society changed.[30]

One of the most effective advocates of the Auburn system was Louis Dwight. Dwight had intended to go into the ministry, but when his lungs were injured he began distributing Bibles for the American Bible Society. He visited several jails in the course of his work and was so concerned over the conditions he found that he formed the Boston Prison Discipline Society. A visit to Auburn sold him on the correctness of its approach. Solitary reflection was not what was needed. Offenders needed hard work and salvation.[31]

In the space of thirty years, the rationale for imprisonment had moved from repentance to discipline and hard work. Hard work meant that the state had a labor force available which could at least defray the cost of their punishment, if not make a profit.[32] This led to protests by labor unions and claims of unfair competition by private businesses. It also led to relaxation of the severe discipline, such as silence, which proved to be counterproductive to the state industries and private contractors employing prisoners.[33]

4. Education and training: the "reformatory" approach. Unfortunately, the Auburn system was not demonstrating desired effects on the prisoners once they were released. Zebulon Brockway, an evangelical Christian converted during one of Charles G. Finney's revivals in the late 1850s,[34] felt that such results proved the need for change.

> I feel that there are very gross defects in the prison system of the land, and that, as a whole, it does not accomplish its design; and that the time has come for reconstruction. There are doubtless in operation in the prisons of this country, religious and moral agencies, physical and hygienic regulations, and a system of employment for prisoners which if combined in the management of one institution, would produce a model prison indeed. To find them, combine them, and apply them, is, in my mind, the great desideratum.[35]

He and others proposed a national conference on prison reform which was conducted in Cincinnati in 1870. The conference was characterized by fervor for the development of prison systems which would reform inmates by creating independent agencies (protected from political interference) responsible for classifying incoming prisoners, and diverting juveniles to separate facilities, incorrigibles to prisons where they would be held for life, and the rest to reformatories where they would work and receive an education. They recommended adoption of the indeterminate sentence (where the judge imposes a minimum and maximum prison term) as a way of restricting release to those prisoners who had reformed.[36]

This marked the beginning of the reformatory movement. The first such prison was Elmira Reformatory in New York, which opened in 1876 with Brockway as its warden. By the 1890s it had become the model for the movement. Its well coordinated discipline, centering around the grading and marking system, was animated by an honest application of the indeterminate sentence. With an industrial activity subordinated to trade and academic schools, and a military organization and calisthenic exercises supplemented by intensive physical culture for defectives, keeping the men fully employed; with the weekly *Summary* for the world's news, and extensive library, and the frequent Sunday lectures by prominent visitors, all prodding the flagging intellect; and above all with the stimulation and kindly encouragement of Professors Monks, Ford, Collin, and Wells, of Dr. Wey, and, last but not least, of Zebulon Brockway—Elmira, "College on the Hill," was surely supplying its inmates with something more to pull on than their own bootstraps when they wished to lift themselves out of the gutter.[37]

Still there were problems. Overcrowding, for example, limited its effectiveness. Brockway complained that filling the facility, designed initially to hold five hundred inmates, to double or triple capacity prevented it from being effective in its purpose of reformation.[38]

And those who followed did not duplicate the comprehensive program of Elmira. In Michigan, for example, the reformatory provided elementary education, but continued to require silence and placed its greatest reliance on hard work.[39] Nonetheless, the reformatory movement caught hold and eventually replaced the Auburn system entirely in the early part of the twentieth century.

5. Diagnosis and treatment: the "correctional" approach. But again, the desired result (reformed prisoners) was not forthcoming. And this stimulated a new movement in criminology, beginning at the end of the nineteenth century and extending through most of the twentieth, which focused on the physical or psychological disabilities of the prisoners. The premise was that most offenders were "sick" in the classic psychiatric sense, and that what was needed was treatment.

This resulted in the medical model of corrections, with its medical experimentation, drugs and psychiatric therapy. To commemorate the change in purpose, prisons were renamed correctional facilities and guards were called correctional officers. Prisoners were called residents. Solitary confinement cells became adjustment centers.[40]

But aside from new names, there was little change. It is estimated that only five per cent of the money spent on prisons was devoted to treatment.[41] Practical matters of prison control and administration often frustrated the treatment programs that did exist. And there was the very real question of whether "treatment" could be done in a coercive environment.

And now treatment, too, has been considered a failure. Norman Carlson, Director of the Federal Bureau of Prisons has said, "I've given up hope for rehabilitation because there is nothing we can do to force change on offenders. Change has got to come from the heart."[42]

Academicians agree. In 1976 a highly influential group of criminal justice professionals stated that rehabilitation no longer worked, and they began to explore new ways of viewing the purposes of punishment.[43]

Conclusion

Criminal justice at one time had focused principally on the need of the offender to restore the victim. This recognized the responsibility of those who cause harm to make good the loss. It also reflected the community awareness that social cohesion required that disputes be dealt with quickly and effectively.

The rise of the modern state inserted new priorities. The new "victim" of crime was the "king's peace," not the person who was actually harmed. Victims desiring restitution could sue in civil court. Over the centuries the imbalance of power between the king and the offender led to a series of technical protections of persons accused of crime or facing punishment.

Criminal justice with a focus on the public peace rather than on restoring the victim involved various efforts to solve the "public" crime problem, principally by separating offenders from the community and attempting to rehabilitate them. The isolation and rehabilitation purposes led to the creation and widespread use of prisons. These have been justified successively as places of penitence, of work and discipline, of general reformation, and of treatment of the criminal. None of these approaches has ever been successfully implemented on a broad scale. But the significance of the redirection of the purpose of criminal justice is profound. Where offenders were once required to compensate the victims or their relatives, now society undertook to cure the offender. Neither the offender nor the state was seen as having responsibility to the victims.

Where does this leave us? There is a current confusion about the appropriate purposes of public justice in dealing with the convicted offender, a process which for brevity I will call punishment. In fact, we see a struggle among concepts of retribution, deterrence, rehabilitation and incapacitation. In the next decade we will need to develop a new model. What will we have to choose from?

Chapter 7

The Purposes of Punishment

My *most unusual* sentencing hearing involved a young man found guilty of armed violence and armed robbery. Tom and his codefendant had been convicted of pistol-whipping and robbing a woman they had picked up outside a bar. She suffered physical injuries which required hospitalization, but left no permanent damage. They were black; she was white. They left her in an alley in the inner city, in the middle of the night, in winter, with no coat. She knocked on several doors pleading for help before a couple let her in, then flagged down a police car which took her to the hospital.

It was a brutal crime. It was also a hard one to understand. Though he had been in trouble once or twice before, always for property offenses, Tom had never been arrested for a violent crime. As I talked with him and with his family, I tried to figure out why he would have done something so out of character and so serious.

During the trial, the woman testified that several times Tom had put his head in her lap, put his arms around her knees and cried, "Mommy! Mommy!" He had not attempted to abuse her sexually.

Before the trial, Tom had been uncooperative. He insisted that he had not kidnaped the woman (one of the charges filed earlier), but was vague about what had happened in the car. After the trial, however, he admitted to me that he had beaten her. He was genuinely sorry for the harm he had caused her. When I again asked him to explain what had been going on that night, he began to open up to me. Based on what he told me, and what I learned from his family, I prepared for the difficult sentencing hearing.

Tom was the son of a biracial marriage. When he was just two, his mother left him, his sister who was two years older and his father. No one had seen her since. His father told me that Tom had frequently asked about his mother as he grew up. He seemed to blame himself for her leaving, as children in broken families often do. Tom became very close to his older sister.

Two weeks before Tom committed this crime, his sister was pushed out of a sixteenth-story window by her boyfriend. They had been arguing, he pushed her, and she fell through the open window to her death. Her boyfriend, who was leader of a gang, threatened the people in the room: he would kill anyone who told the police what he had done. As a result, they corroborated his story that she had committed suicide. One of the witnesses told the family the true story, but refused to go with them to the police to press murder charges against the boyfriend.

After a memorial service in their church, Tom and his family were confronted by the boyfriend and his gang. Several of them had weapons. The next day they came to Tom's house and again threatened the family with reprisals if they persisted in going to the police.

Tom was in turmoil. The police had not followed up, and his father insisted that they let the matter rest so that no one else would be hurt.

Tom was not willing to accept this decision, but it seemed there was little he could do.

On the night of the crime, Tom drove to his friend's (the codefendant's) house. He asked him for a handgun, not really sure whether he wanted it for his family's protection or for revenge on the boyfriend. He put the gun under the front seat, and they began driving around. After an hour or so they saw the woman coming out of a bar and picked her up.

During the next forty-five minutes, Tom became increasingly agitated. He asked her why she had not come to the burial or memorial service. He wept. He put his face in her lap and called her Mommy. At that point, he later told me, he believed that she was his mother. And when the woman insisted she knew nothing about his sister's death and was unable to comfort him, he became angry. He took the pistol, beat her, and left her in the alley.

The trial was over, so there was no opportunity to present a defense of insanity or temporary insanity. But this was what I presented to the judge at the sentencing. It did not excuse his behavior. But it did show that this was an uncharacteristic act, committed under unusual circumstances at a time of tremendous emotional turmoil. It was very unlikely that he would ever commit such a crime again.

The law in that state required the judge to send Tom to prison for at least six years. The question was, What sentence ought he to impose? The woman had agreed to get into the car, but certainly had not agreed to being beaten. What kind of sentence is appropriate in this situation?

Before I tell you what this judge did, let's look at the underlying issue. The question criminologists ask, usually in the tranquillity of a classroom, is, What role can punishment play in reducing crime? It is the same question that judges, prosecutors and defense attorneys deal with in busy courtrooms where thousands of men and women are sentenced every day. The question has few satisfying answers and no clear ones.

Theories of the Causes of Crime

The *punishment* of crime is often governed by what we see as the *cause* of crime. We saw in the last chapter that there have been two major schools of thought. The utilitarian school focuses on the need to deter crime by making punishment quick, certain and severe enough to offset the "pleasures" a potential criminal anticipates from committing a crime. The other school begins with the assumption that factors out of the control of the criminal contribute to the decision to commit a crime. This school sees punishment as the state's way of addressing those factors. An ultimate objective of both is to reduce crime.

American criminal justice thinking has been predominantly of the second school. And with this school five more-or-less distinct theories of the cause of crime have arisen: the constitutional, the geographic, the economic, the sociologic and the psychiatric.[1]

What seems apparent as one examines these views is that each offers plausible explanations for at least some offenders some of the time. And so most criminologists hold to a multiple causation theory:

After examining much of the research and conclusions of the behavioral scientists (including the geographical and economic determinists) over the past two hundred years, the only honest conclusion is that thus far no unitary cause for crime has been found. Each discipline, through careful research, throws considerable light on the perplexing subject but each of their conclusions can be regarded only as segmental.[2]

The significance of the multiple causation theory is that it recognizes that criminal behavior is not totally determined. Individuals do differ in the likelihood that they will engage in criminal behavior, in part because of constitutional, geographic, economic and other factors. Society must consider these factors when deciding how to respond to crime.

But as the research team of psychiatrist Samuel Yochelson and psychologist Stanton Samenow concluded after a sixteen-year study, not all people who are economically deprived commit crimes.[3] Nor do all of those who grow up in deprived circumstances. Some who have not experienced those kinds of deprivations *do* commit crimes. They concluded that *criminals* are the major cause of crime, not society. We must keep this in mind as we consider how to deal with a wrongdoer.

In Defense of Punishment

Punishment is the deliberate infliction of pain. Because of this, some have said that it is an inappropriate sanction. We should want to help people, they say, not deliberately hurt them. The harm that they have caused others is not lessened in any way by making them suffer too.

> Punishment essentially involves the deliberate infliction of suffering. Not only that, the suffering is imposed precisely because it is suffering and not, as in medicine or education, as an unavoidable side effect of a practice that is supposed to be directed to the welfare of the persons subjected to it.[4]

Now if that is true, that for no reason other than to show our dislike we inflict pain on those who have hurt us, there is certainly a problem with the justice of punishment. And if we are honest, we will admit that *part* of our desire for "justice" comes from our desire to see our enemies hurt. We need to deal appropriately with our desire for revenge and to watch carefully whether the kinds and the extent of punishment we permit are derived from justice or from vengeful feelings.

But it does not follow that punishment should be avoided. Punishment accomplishes several things.[5] First, it emphasizes that we are all part of a community, and it helps define the values that we live by.[6] Certain behavior is wrong, and we expect this to be taught in churches, families, schools and other institutions in society. When we punish lawbreakers we reinforce these institutions.

Second, we say to the offender and to the community that we believe in both freedom of choice and responsibility, and that we will respect freedom by punishing those who violate the law. We see this at the international level in calls for sanctions against countries which are not respecting the human rights of their own citizens or neighbors. If countries have "free will," why do we assume that people do not? And if they do, isn't punishment an appropriate way to recognize that?

Third, we say to offenders that we believe they are capable of changing, and that it is important that *they choose* to change. To do this requires that we treat the individual not as a means to an end, but as someone with innate value, and whose value we want to preserve and enhance. This means that punishment should be a solemn and sad event, not a time for celebration and delight (thinking of the celebrations which have taken place in some states at executions).

I am not justifying the kind of punishments we inflict today in prison. It should be apparent that prison may convey other more powerful and generally destructive messages to prisoners. But we should not abandon the notion of punishment simply because there are problems with its implementation. Perhaps what we need are new (or old and mislaid) forms of punishment that serve other purposes.[7]

Purposes of Punishment
How then do we determine the appropriate form of punishment? What purposes *should* the sentence serve? Answers to these questions have traditionally fallen into three categories: deterrence, rehabilitation and incapacitation.

1. Deterrence. One of the most commonly held purposes, discussed briefly in the last chapter, is deterrence. This argument assumes that people are rational and have free will. It is obviously not possible to deter those who do not care about the consequences or those who, knowing the consequences, are yet incapable of acting in any other way.

As Beccaria demonstrated two hundred years ago, people are deterred only if they see the likely punishment as outweighing the likely benefits of their actions. As a result, an unlikely punishment will not deter significantly, even if it is a catastrophic one. And a likely punishment may not deter if the benefits are even more likely and far greater than the possible punishment.

Chuck Colson tells of a man who sold narcotics in New York State when it had a well-publicized law mandating a fifteen-to-life sentence for anyone convicted of selling narcotics.[8] He asked the man how he could be so foolish as to commit the crime with that kind of sentence hanging over his head. The man told him that he had worked on a construction crew building the World Trade Center. He was paid $720 per week, and if he fell he would die. Dealing drugs he could make $300,000 in a week, and if he got caught he faced only imprisonment. He played the odds and got caught.

Most of us at one time or another have probably chosen not to commit a crime for fear of being caught and punished. Deterrence is an important and valuable function of punishment. But it has limitations.

One is that it is virtually impossible to prove that high penalties deter better than less severe penalties. A panel of the National Academy of Sciences conducted an exhaustive review of the available research on deterrence. It concluded that the evidence did not justify drawing any strong conclusions about whether it works or not.[9] Arguments for or against deterrence are basically anecdotal and inconclusive. Prisons are filled with people who were not deterred, nor were the hundreds of thousands of people who were convicted and put on probation. There is virtually no way of identifying the people who decided not to commit a crime primarily because of the possible punishment. So deterrence is a theory which may well be true, but cannot be proven.

Second, many crimes are committed by people who do not take the time to consider the consequences. For example, the FBI reports that over fifty-five per cent of all homicides are committed by a relative or acquaintance of the victim, usually in the course of an argument. Relatively few homicides are premeditated, which is a prerequisite for deterrence.[10]

Crimes other than murder are often done either in the heat of the moment (for example, assault committed during an argument), or in a situation which escalates quickly into a crime or a more serious crime. For example, a person who decides to hold up a store may do that with a gun because he assumes that it will ensure quick compliance with his demands and therefore reduce the likelihood that he will be caught. If the storekeeper resists, the robber may end up shooting in order to get away, something he should have anticipated when he began the crime, but which he probably did not even consider.

A third problem with deterrence is that we have placed too much of the burden on the severity of punishment. As Beccaria told us, this is a risky tactic. If the punishment is too severe, the offender may actually be tempted to commit more serious offenses to avoid capture (as in the example above). And judges and juries may be reluctant to convict if they feel the sentence will be too severe.

Some states have attempted to deal with this problem by mandating sentences for people convicted of certain crimes. When they discovered that prosecutors were reducing the charges in some cases in order to obtain a conviction without the severe sentence, laws were passed which prohibited reducing the charges. Massachusetts, for example, enacted a gun statute which mandated a one-year prison sentence for anyone convicted of illegal possession of a firearm. Prosecutors were required to file charges every time there was an arrest, and they were prohibited from reducing the charges. A subsequent study showed that the discretion had dropped to another level: eighty-nine per cent of the police officers surveyed said that they had changed their approach to people they suspected of carrying weapons illegally: they no longer stop and search (for weapons) anyone they feel is "otherwise innocent."[11]

Fourth, deterrence is an inadequate guide, by itself, to the amount of punishment that should be imposed. The logic of deterrence is that people will see what happened to someone who committed the crime they are considering and will decide not to risk such a fate themselves. This would suggest that extreme punishments would be most effective because they would raise the stakes. But is it just to punish one person in an extreme way to deter another person?

In the 1800s England had one hundred sixty crimes punishable by hanging, including ones as trivial as stealing a loaf of bread. In one month, there were over forty executions each day. But crime did not drop. In fact, people who gathered to watch the hanging of a pickpocket lost their wallets to other pickpockets working the crowd.[12]

Still, these limitations do not mean that deterrence is not a valid purpose of punishment. Scripture talks about the deterrent value of punishment in certain cases. Interestingly, they are always cases which involve premeditation.[13] But we should not rely too heavily on deterrence to stop crime, nor should we set extremely high sentences in the hope that they will deter. Any punishment imposed swiftly and certainly may deter other would-be offenders. It is difficult to say much more than that.

2. *Rehabilitation.* A second purpose for punishment is rehabilitation. As we saw in the last chapter, the history of American prisons has centered around the idea of segregating criminals and doing something with them to make them better. The treatment has been coercive: they have had no choice about being in the prison, and the length of their sentence was determined by how much they improved. We also saw that each theory ended in failure and was replaced by a new strategy in what was essentially a futile task: to take a large number of offenders from a variety of backgrounds, require them to participate in certain programs to the extent that the security concerns of the administration and the budget would permit, and expect that there would be significant improvement.

Treatment programs can be divided into two types: those which deal with offenders as individuals, and those which deal with them as a group. The first has followers in the constitutional and psychiatric schools. The second has followers in the sociological, geographical and economic schools. Rehabilitation has gotten a bad reputation in the last ten years. It has been criticized on two levels—it doesn't work, and it isn't right. Let's look at each.

In 1974, criminologist Robert Martinson wrote that based on an extensive survey of 231 rehabilitation program studies conducted from 1945 to 1967, he had to conclude that "nothing works."[14] Programs which were claiming success in the treatment of offenders were actually no better, and in some cases even worse, than no treatment at all.

His statement was challenged vigorously, and he retreated from his absolute repudiation of rehabilitation. He did concede that individual programs may work with certain kinds of offenders, and he maintained that programs should be made available for those inmates who could benefit from them and wanted them. But the idea of sending people to prison to make them better persons was simply a mistake.

Now there are various explanations for this conclusion. One is that the idea of rehabilitation simply does not have merit. It was a bad idea from the outset. But others assert that we have never really tried to treat offenders. Rehabilitation programs have always been underfunded and have competed with security concerns. If the prison is overcrowded, then the classroom and vocational training areas and sometimes even the chapel are converted into dormitories. If there are too few guards to escort prisoners to certain programs, then they just don't go.

Both explanations have some truth to them. We certainly expected too much of rehabilitation. The goals of the proponents were ambitious, but no program will change someone who does not want to change.

And it is clear that in spite of the millions of dollars invested in rehabilitation programs, the total investment was minimal compared to other priorities. One would certainly expect more than five per cent of the total budget of something we call correctional facilities to go toward rehabilitation programs. Few of us would stay at a hospital which devoted that little money to medical treatment.

But there have been successes.[15] Rehabilitation programs that work appear to follow three broad guidelines:[16] First, in more successful programs no one form of treatment is considered the only treatment. A variety of interventions are used. Second, such programs focus on those types of offenders who will benefit most from the specific treatment, recognizing that not all will respond favorably.[17] Third, the programs that work are the ones that deal with how the offender relates in a group, rather than those which deal with the offender through psychiatric counseling. In other words, rehabilitation that focuses on the individual in isolation does not work, whereas rehabilitation programs involving modifying behavior, changing attitudes, or developing interpersonal or vocational skills *do* work.

There is another question which must be asked, however, related to the *justice* of the rehabilitation model: Is it *just* to send someone to prison to coerce them to change? We may talk in terms of treatment, and have benign motives, but the question remains: Assuming that we have the power to change offenders, should we exercise it?

Initially this sounds silly. Of course we should rehabilitate people. It is good for society since we do not have to worry about the person committing new crimes, and it is good for the individual, since he or she will function in a more socially acceptable way and be happier.

But C. S. Lewis has pointed out that as offensive as the idea of punishment may be to the advocates of rehabilitation, whatever rehabilitation is being done to the offender is still compulsory. The question is, What limits should be placed on the compulsion? Those who believe in rehabilitation will want the criminal to get whatever is needed in order to change him. There are no upper limits to the coercion he faces. If it takes one person three times as long to be treated as it does another, that is fine. No matter that both committed the same crime.[18] Those who do not believe rehabilitation should be the guiding principle respond that the criminal should get what the crime deserves and no more.

Perhaps we can understand the proper role of rehabilitation programs if we distinguish between what have been called "state enforced rehabilitation" and "state provided rehabilitation."[19] State *enforced* participation in rehabilitation programs is what Lewis warned against. It not only is of questionable value, it raises serious ethical questions. But state *provided* programs should be available to offenders who want to take advantage of them. Rehabilitation in a nondeterministic framework says that people who want to climb out of a hole need ladders. We cannot make people climb them, but we can and should make them available.

3. Incapacitation. The third rationale for punishment is incapacitation, which simply means preventing offenders from committing new crimes. Prisoners and probationers are limited in their ability to break the law. They are incapacitated.

Recently incapacitation has received a great deal of attention by criminologists. A considerable amount of work has been done to determine factors for predicting whether someone is likely to commit new crimes. Some have thought that if we cannot rehabilitate, we can at least detain the most "crime prone" longer than we might have otherwise and reduce the number of crimes that they are free to commit.

The idea of predicting future criminality was a part of the rehabilitative model.[20] In rehabilitation, offenders are kept until they are "well," which means until they are unlikely to commit new crimes. The decision is an *individual* one, based on each person's adjustment to prison, response to the various treatment programs, and so on.

Recently, statisticians have been attempting to see whether it is possible to identify *classes* of persons who are likely to commit new crimes. They have focused on juvenile records, use of illegal drugs currently and as a juvenile, imprisonment for more than fifty per cent of the last two years, and previous convictions for the present offense as significant predictive factors.[21]

But this work has been plagued with the problem of overpredicting, that is, identifying people as likely to commit new crimes who in fact do not do so. And so while some studies have claimed an eighty-two per cent success rate,[22] what they mean is that eighty-two per cent of the people who commit new crimes were people they predicted would do so. Unfortunately, other researchers have shown that for every person predicted to commit new crimes who does actually break the law there are *two* people who were also predicted to commit new offenses who don't.[23] It reminds me of the state lottery ads which say that you can't win if you don't play. That's true, of course, but it does not mean that everyone who plays is likely to win. (Although that is the impression the ad wants to give.) Researchers have been able to identify factors that describe the people who will commit new crimes, but those factors describe an even greater number of people who will not get into trouble.

Now this may simply be a matter of incomplete research. We may discover a foolproof way to identify the people who will commit new crimes. If so, how should we use that information?

This is now a matter of great debate among criminologists because it raises tremendous ethical issues. Should we penalize people for what we believe they will do? This could mean giving someone a long sentence for a minor crime because our computers tell us that he will commit many serious crimes if we let him out. Is this just?

If our goal is to reduce crime at all costs, then such a sentence is justified. But most of us would agree that there are other important societal goals which must be considered. If we punish people because we believe they have free choice, then we need to understand that there is always the possibility of choosing to change. Christians, who believe in the importance and reality of repentance and conversion, certainly understand this. We cannot give up on anyone. Second, there must be limits to the amount of punishment that we give, and those limits ought to be based on what the person has done, not what we think they may do in the future.

In my experience as a trial attorney, it became obvious that incapacitation was a very important consideration to judges in sentencing. Their decisions about the likelihood of new crimes were mostly intuitive, based on their observation of the defendants' criminal records and the crimes in question. Consequently, a great deal of informal selective incapacitation is going on already, but without any way of scientifically testing whether the judges' hunches are right.

Increasing numbers of state legislatures have passed habitual offender laws, which mandate prison sentences for people who have been convicted of multiple crimes.[24] This is an effort to get those who are frequent offenders off the street and into prison.

The public has a right to be protected. But our prisons are filled to capacity, often because we have sent people there who are not likely to commit new crimes or because we have made it impossible to release early those who have demonstrated that they have changed. That is a mistake.

On the other hand, most would agree that prison is where we should put a person who is likely to continue preying on the public. His sentence length should be based on the crime he was convicted of, but he should serve that sentence in prison.

There is a related issue. Given the large number of "false positives"—people predicted to continue breaking the law who in fact do not—any policy to lock up those classes of expected offenders would significantly raise the prison population without significantly lowering the crime rate. Three studies which considered the effect of giving five-year sentences to everyone convicted of a felony found that the crime rate would drop between ten and twenty per cent but that the prison population would at least triple in size and perhaps grow over five hundred per cent.[25]

An alternative approach is to use the prediction data to identify the persons least likely to commit new crimes, and make sure that they are not sentenced to prison terms unless that is indicated because of one of the other purposes of punishment. This would raise some of the same ethical questions, but would have the advantage of being a mitigating factor, rather than an aggravating one. It would also conserve scarce prison space by removing the people whose detention seems least necessary to protect the public.

What Should We Do with Tom?

Now let us return to my client, who is awaiting sentencing for his violent crime. What should the judge do with Tom? What purpose or combination of purposes should govern that decision?

Deterrence is certainly a factor. But should the judge give Tom sixty years just to send a message to the streets? Is that fair to Tom or to the rest of us who have to pay his room and board? Is there any evidence that potential criminals in the streets will ever hear about the sentence?

Rehabilitation could undoubtedly take place outside of prison. Tom needs help in dealing with his mother's abandonment. Is he likely to get that in prison? Or will he be debilitated by a lengthy prison sentence?

Retribution is certainly important. Tom, in spite of his problems, still had the capacity to choose how he would behave. Does this help determine what form the punishment should take?

Incapacitation is perhaps unnecessary. Tom had never done anything like this before. The crime was triggered by an event that could not be duplicated—his sister was the only other child of his parent's marriage, and the circumstances surrounding her death and funeral were certainly unique. On the other hand, now that he has committed such a crime, can we be sure that he will not repeat it, that he will indeed receive the help he needs?

If the decision is hard for you, imagine what it is like for judges who have to make such decisions every day. And realize when you read sensational crime stories in the newspaper that the defendants who have committed crimes like Tom's are not monsters, even though their offenses were monstrous. They are human beings.

Frankly, I did not believe that Tom needed to be sent to prison to protect the public. He could have been given a long term of probation with intensive community supervision. He could have been ordered to pay the victim for her losses and her medical treatment (including psychiatric counseling if that were needed to help her recover). He could have been required to obtain counseling himself to learn to deal with the loss of his mother and sister.

On the other hand, the offense was a very serious one. The victim could have died of exposure in the frigid weather. And state law required a prison sentence. The codefendant, who had clearly been less involved in the crime, had already been sentenced to eight years. The prosecutor was demanding a sixty-year sentence, the maximum allowed in that state. I recommended twelve.

The judge, after considerable thought, sentenced Tom to serve sixteen years in prison.

Conclusion

At the end of part I we noted that there were three parties affected by a criminal act: the victim, the offender and the surrounding community. In part II we have traced the development of the criminal justice system and the changing rationales for punishing offenders. What has happened?

The first step in the development of a "system" came when the community outlawed blood feuds. The victim and offender (and their families) had treated offenses as entirely familial matters, but the effect of the feuds on the community was too disruptive. So the early law codes limited blood feuds, but held the offender responsible to the victim by requiring restitution payments.

The growth of the modern state, competing for power with both local authorities and the church, led to a total redefinition of the injury. It was no longer a wrong against the victim; it was a crime against the state, against the "king's peace."

There are two ways to understand this development. One is that the state became a fourth party affected by the crime. The other is that the state replaced the victim and the community, with the result that there are now only two parties: the state and the offender. Under legal theory and in practice, the second is clearly what has happened. The victim is simply part of the prosecution's case, and the community is involved only indirectly by electing officials who pass laws and administer the criminal justice system, or by various means of self-help (from locks to neighborhood watch programs to vigilantism).

But the reality of crime is that the victim and community *are* affected. The wounds are real. The criminal justice system is unable to deal with them because it has removed them as active participants with legitimate interests. It has instead focused its energies on the offenders, first protecting them from abuse of the state's power and then experimenting with ways of reducing crime by changing the offenders and deterring other potential criminals.

Rehabilitation and deterrence are limited in their effectiveness. Increasingly, the state has relied on incapacitation in its attempt to solve the crime problem. Its successes have been limited at best.

The state has assumed complete responsibility for crime control. It focuses on future crime, attempting to prevent it by terror and force. As a result, we have cast aside a number of tools that could be available to us (as we will see in part IV) and relied solely on the state's power. There are dangers in this approach.

How else could we deal with crime? As Christians do we have unique insights we can offer to our society? Can Scripture help us find new direction to solving an old problem?

Part III

How Can Scripture Help Us?

Chapter 8

The Mosaic Law

As *Moses ascended* Mount Sinai, smoke billowed and the mountain shook. A cloud covered the mountain. A trumpet blast rang out. Moses, Israel's representative, spoke and God answered in thunder, descending onto the mountain. There, after forty days and nights, he gave Moses the Law.

It is important to note several things about the Law in Israel's life. First, it was given to them only *after* an act of redemption, their deliverance from slavery in Egypt. The Pentateuch is full of this reminder, and the Ten Commandments themselves begin with it: "I am the LORD your God, who brought you out of Egypt, out of the land of slavery" (Ex 20:2). The people agreed that they would do everything that their Deliverer commanded.

Second, the Law which Moses was given comprised the terms of a covenant. Historians tell us that the agreement between God and the people of Israel was a kind of covenant the Israelites would have been familiar with: a "suzerain-vassal" treaty. In this relationship, the all-powerful suzerain (overlord) agrees to extend benefits to the weaker, dependent vassal (servant), and the vassal promises to meet the conditions established by the suzerain.[1] The covenant, in short, was not a "social contract" between equals.

Third, and equally important, the Law was not a *condition* of God's grace or redemption. God made a covenant with Israel and gave them his Law *despite* their having already spectacularly proven (in the golden-calf incident) their disobedience and rebellion. The covenant was made with both parties knowing that Israel was a treacherous and unworthy partner (Deut 9:6—10:5). With this in mind we can understand how the terms of the covenant—the Law—are not threats but positive instruction in life. Or, as Moses said of the Law on the very banks of the Jordan, "They are not just idle words for you—they are your life. By them you will live" (Deut 32:47).

Can Scripture Help Us?

When we look at the Law we find a detailed collection of legal provisions which cover virtually all possible aspects of Israelite life. (Note: Throughout this section the upper-case word *Law* refers to the terms of the Sinai covenant and its additions and development in the Pentateuch. Reference to all other legal codes and systems is made with lower-case *law*.) Because it was part of a suzerain-vassal treaty, its terms had to be specific—in order to be obedient, the vassals needed to know exactly what was required of them. So rather than laying down general principles of behavior ("treat each other fairly"), the Ten Commandments gave specific instructions such as "Thou shalt not steal." But the Law goes even beyond this to particular examples: "If a man grazes his livestock in a field or vineyard and lets them stray and they graze in another man's field, he must make restitution from the best of his own field or vineyard" (Ex 22:5).

Now few of us confront the problem of livestock grazing in a neighbor's fields. The very specificity which made the covenant helpful to Israel presents problems for us. And what about provisions like the requirement that the death penalty be imposed on anyone who worked on the sabbath? Do we apply only the parts that "feel" relevant to us, ignoring the parts that don't? Do we try to enact the whole Law, word for word, through our legislatures? Or do we throw out the whole thing as unworkable and uninstructive?

We have just run into two major difficulties which theologians call the problems of *contextualization* and *particularity*.[2] The Law was given in a specific *context*—several thousand years ago—to a select nation with a unique relationship to God, a nation which ceased to exist as an independent state centuries before the birth of Christ. And it was *particular* to that nation, as we have seen, responding to specific issues growing out of that context.

The New Testament *context* is closer to our own. The judicial code was enacted by a government which did not have a unique relationship with God. But the Gospels and epistles are not *particular* in critiquing Roman law and administration. Their references to the criminal justice system are more oblique and virtually always concern Christians being tried for their Christian witness under Roman law or Jesus' response to Pharisaic application of the Old Testament Law. We can learn a great deal about how individual Christians should respond to crime and to official injustice, and we also learn about the role of government (even pagan government). But it tells us very little about the specific conduct that nations ought to prohibit, or about the purposes and forms of punishment that may be imposed.

If the Law given to Israel was part of an exclusive relationship with God, what relevance does it have for us? What can we learn from the New Testament, in which Christians were more likely to be defendants than judges, prosecutors, defense attorneys or lawmakers? Can we gain any insight from Scripture on how to respond to crime today?

Can Scripture, which we hold to be authoritative over all of life,* help us respond to the dilemmas our criminal justice system faces?

The Law as Paradigm

It was the sabbath. Jesus, entering the synagogue to teach, noticed a woman who had been crippled for eighteen years. We are told that a spirit had oppressed her, making it impossible for her to straighten up. She walked around bent over (Lk 13:10-17).

What should Jesus do? The Ten Commandments prohibited any work on the sabbath. The penalty for violating it was death. Over the centuries, a number of rabbinic interpretations had attempted to clarify just what constituted "work." Apparently none of these addressed healing. Jesus had gotten in trouble before with the religious leaders for his acts of mercy on the sabbath. What would he do?

He called the woman before the congregation, told her she was set free, and laid his hands on her. Immediately she was healed.

The ruler of the synagogue was indignant. To him, healing was work, and the people should come to Jesus on one of the other six days if they wanted to be made whole.

Jesus challenged that view: "You hypocrites! Doesn't each of you on the Sabbath untie his ox or donkey from the stall and lead it out to give it water? Then should not this woman, a daughter of Abraham, whom Satan has kept bound for eighteen long years, be set free on the Sabbath day from what bound her?"

We are told that the woman praised God, the people were delighted, and his opponents were humiliated because they could not answer his argument.

Although Jesus lived in a country which had been taken over and

---

*We believe that the Bible is God's authoritative and inspired Word. It is without error in all its teaching, including creation, history, its own origins, and salvation. Christians must submit to its divine authority, both individually and corporately, in all matters of belief and conduct, which is demonstrated by true righteous living.—from the statement of faith, Prison Fellowship Ministries.

annexed by a foreign power, he did not ignore the teaching of the Law. He taught it, he lived by it, he insisted that he was not abolishing it—not even the least significant part would pass away until all things had been accomplished.

But *righteousness* was greater than the mere legalistic obedience to the Law which characterized the Pharisees (Mt 5:17-20).

Jesus had not disregarded the Law. Rather, he had understood its *meaning* and was not bound by restrictive legalism. This is an illustration of using the Law as a *paradigm*. A paradigm is a model. It shows how an underlying principle works out in a specific instance.

The advantage of viewing the Law as a paradigm is that we are forced to treat it not merely as an ancient collection of legal matter, but as a model which we must emulate. It helps us to accept the universal application of the Law and to be challenged and guided by it without either stumbling over the problem of particularity or failing to adequately recognize the problem of contextualization.

Thus the context and the particulars of the Law—and of the prophets, the wisdom books and the New Testament—become the very components we need in order to allow Scripture to inform our thinking about how twentieth-century America should respond to its criminal justice problems. They supply what we need in order to consider the Law as a concrete example of how God dealt with a specific people at a specific time to establish a just and righteous nation.[3]

So we do not look at the Law with the expectation that we can or should enact it directly through our legislatures. Instead we derive its significance for us through a series of steps:

1. Understand its context.

2. Ask ourselves how theology understands and informs the passages we are examining.

3. Look at the Law itself, together with comparable passages of Scripture where the underlying purposes or principles are more explicit, as well as contemporaneous extrabiblical resources.

4. Identify the principles behind the particular passages we are studying. We are looking for principles which lie between the general theological understanding of "justice," for example, and the specific, concrete regulations that appear in the Law.[4]

This gives us a way to study the one time when God instructed a nation in how it should deal with what we now call criminal cases (among other aspects of national life), and take from that study principles we can use to critique and modify our own system of justice.

The Universal Character of the Law

As we will see in the next chapter, justice is a fundamental dimension of God's own character (Deut 10:17-18; Is 61:8; Jer 22:3; Ps 37:28; 89:14; Mic 6:8; Mt 23:23). As a result, justice is inherent in the cosmic order which he created. Paul tells us that God's divine nature is plain in creation, and it may be seen by those willing to look for it (Rom 1:18-20). For this reason, God's judgment against all people—Jews and Gentiles—is just (Rom 2:1-11).

What place, then, does the Law have in revealing that underlying cosmic order? The Law was part of a suzerain-vassal treaty entered into immediately after God had redeemed the people of Israel from oppression. The Law was given in the context of an exclusive relationship between God and a chosen people.

And yet they discovered almost immediately that the Law also was to have universal implications. In the offer that God first made when Israel camped beneath Mt. Sinai, he referred to a unique role that the nation would play among other nations. They were not simply his chosen people. They were to be a kingdom of priests and a holy nation (Ex 19:6), with the responsibility of showing other nations the character and demands of the one true God. Ultimately, they were to be the agent of redemption for all the earth (cf. Gen 12:3).

This meant that the ethical demands of the Law were intended by God (and were understood by the people of Israel) to be universal. *Righteousness* and *justice* had meaning because of the character of God, and thus (because God is the Creator of all nations) had meaning to all nations. This is why Abraham could confidently ask, "Will not the Judge of all the earth do right?" (Gen 18:25).

It also explains why the prophets did not limit their scope to the (then) splintered nation which had received the Law, but condemned the practices of surrounding countries as well.

I will punish the world for its evil,
the wicked for their sins. (Is 13:11)

The prophets warned of God's judgment against Philistia, Edom, Moab, Ammon, Egypt, Assyria, Damascus, Tyre, Babylon and Nineveh. (See Jer 45—51; Ezek 25—32; Dan 2 and 7; Amos 3; Obadiah; Jonah; and Nahum.)

Isaiah offered an eschatological view of this universal purpose of Israel and the Law:

In the last days
the mountain of the LORD's temple
    will be established
    as chief among the mountains;
it will be raised above the hills,
    and all nations will stream to it.

Many peoples will come and say,
"Come, let us go up to the mountain
    of the LORD,
    to the house of the God of Jacob.
He will teach us his ways,
    so that we may walk in his paths."
The Law will go out from Zion,
    the word of the LORD from Jerusalem.
He will judge between the nations
    and will settle disputes for many peoples.
They will beat their swords into plowshares

> and their spears into pruning hooks.
> Nation will not take up sword against nation,
>   nor will they train for war anymore. (Is 2:2-4; see also 42:1-4)

This understanding of the Law was not limited to the Old Testament people. Jesus, the promised Messiah, came at a time when the nation had been conquered and annexed by a gentile nation. Nevertheless he stated that not one letter of the Law would disappear until "everything is accomplished" (Mt 5:17-18).

In his letter to the gentile Christians at Rome, Paul conducted an extensive discussion of the role of the Law. He did not conclude that it is irrelevant in the Christian era. On the contrary, he said that the purpose of the Law is to make us all conscious of sin (Rom 3:20). He went on to show that righteousness comes by faith in Christ, not by following the Law—not because the Law is of no effect, but because it condemns any who violate it, and "all have sinned and fall short of the glory of God" (Rom 3:23).[5] If the Law did not have universal application, Paul would not have made this argument. What he opposed was the effort to obtain righteousness by following the Law, since that was not only futile but also a failure to accept the redemption which God offered through Christ.

The Law, then, was offered to a particular people at a specific point in history. But viewing the Law as paradigm helps us understand its universality. Its principles had broad application. Those who violated the just and righteous demands expressed in the Law, whether they were Israelites, surrounding nations or Christians in the church at Rome, were subject to judgment. Redemption comes, as it always has, through the gracious intervention of God himself.

> Two things persuade me that at least some of the ancient commandments embody moral laws that we do consult as a source of God's will. First is the identity of the commander: the God who commanded is the same as the God who created. A purposeful creator, planning a world of rational beings, would have some sort

of design for their development as a human community. And if he wills that his people live by that design, would his commandments not embody that will?

The second reason lies in the commands themselves; some of God's commands simply force us to see that they are for everyone on his earth.[6]

Lewis Smedes, who wrote these words, has touched on the second and third steps of our process of applying biblical teaching to today's issues: consideration of the underlying theology, and examination of the Law itself. And that is what we will do in the next two chapters, concluding with an analysis of the principles demonstrated by the Law as paradigm.

Chapter 9

Justice and Righteousness

When *I was twelve* years old our family watched very little television. But we did watch "Perry Mason." In fact, my views of the criminal justice system were dramatically affected by that program.

Perry Mason never lost a case, and not just because he was a skillful lawyer. His clients were never guilty. In the face of a seemingly irrefutable prosecution case, his logical mind would discern tiny flaws in the evidence, and with the dogged detective work of private investigator Paul Drake, he would break through the deception and reveal the true offender.

Normally the case was resolved during the trial. Perry Mason's cross-examination skills were matchless, and on most occasions he caused the true criminal to confess under his relentless questioning, to the disgust and disappointment of prosecutor Hamilton Burger.

After the satisfying denouement, in which he explained to confused
and admiring costars Paul Drake and Della Street just how he had
identified the true criminal, the credits would run. In the background
was the familiar symbol of the Greek goddess Justicia, with her blindfold, scales and sword.

Impartial Justicia, weighing the evidence and ready to impose judgment on the wrongdoer. Impersonal, objective, single-minded, relentless, fair.

This represented to me the ideal, what our criminal justice system
was striving for. Then I became a lawyer and discovered that reality
did not match "Perry Mason." Not all defendants are innocent. Few
attorneys are as skillful as Perry Mason. Many of our criminal cases
seem to focus more on the technical rights of defendants than on the
issue of guilt or innocence. Wealthy defendants with high-priced legal
help have a decided advantage over poor defendants. Some guilty
offenders are acquitted; innocent defendants are occasionally convicted. Victims are forgotten and angry. The goddess's blindfold sometimes appears to be preventing her from seeing the truth rather than
enabling her to be impartial.

Not only do we fail to meet the ideal of Justicia, but as I studied
Scripture, I discovered that the biblical concept of justice is much
different and even more foreign to modern Americans. Far from
being impartial, it reflects special concern for protecting vulnerable
people from victimization by the powerful. Justice is so closely linked
with the concepts of righteousness and peace that the three often
merge. It brings judgment on the wrongdoer but also works to restore
the victim, the offender and the community. And most important, it
stems not from the image of a minor Greek goddess, but from the
character of the one true God, Jehovah.

God Is the Source

The Old Testament understanding of justice and righteousness begins with the realization that these principles are dimensions of God's

character, not external standards which the Almighty for some reason is compelled to obey. They are a part of his character. Therefore, if he were to act unjustly or unrighteously he would not be himself (Gen 18:25; Deut 32:3-4).

In fact, God's mighty deeds were acknowledged even by other nations to be just and righteous. Pharaoh confessed to Moses: "This time I have sinned. . . . The LORD is in the right, and I and my people are in the wrong" (Ex 9:27).

God's righteousness and justice were demonstrated in at least three ways: in his redemptive acts, in his Law and in punishment.

Redemptive acts. The account of God's relationship with the people of Israel centers around his mighty act of redemption in the exodus. The Israelites had been enslaved in Egypt, and after four hundred years of increasing oppression, they cried out to God for relief. He responded by demonstrating his power over the spiritual and military forces of the Egyptians, and bringing his people out of Egypt. He immediately made it clear that he expected them to reflect his character (Lev 19:2).[1]

Those who knew God were those who recognized that "I am the LORD, who exercises kindness, justice and righteousness on earth" (Jer 9:24). But that recognition was not to be static. It produced imitation, so that defending the poor and needy was actually defined as knowing God (Jer 22:16). Acting justly and righteously is *both* a way of knowing the just and righteous God *and* a response to that knowledge.

This is underscored in the demand of the covenant, the suzerain-vassal treaty, that the people of Israel "follow justice and justice alone, so that you may live and possess the land the LORD your God is giving you" (Deut 16:20).

The Law. The source of the Law was God, not secular rulers (Is 33:22). Moses emphasized this as he reviewed the Law at the end of his life:

What other nation is so great as to have their gods near them the way the LORD our God is near us whenever we pray to him? And what other nation is so great as to have such righteous decrees and laws as this body of laws I am setting before you today? (Deut 4:7-8)[2]

Even those in authority were subject to the Law since it reflected the character of God, not the character (and self-interest) of a given king (Ps 119:137-44).[3]

King David wrote a remarkable psalm on the Law. Psalm 119 is filled with praise for the righteous Laws which God had given and on which David meditated:

I will praise you with an upright heart
    as I learn your righteous laws. . . .
At midnight I rise to give you thanks
    for your righteous laws. . . .
Your statutes are forever right;
    give me understanding that I may live. . . .
All your words are true;
    all your righteous laws are eternal. . . .
May my tongue sing of your word,
    for all your commands are righteous. (vv. 7, 62, 144, 160, 172)

David was king, but he acknowledged that the Law came from God.

Punishment. Any discussion of the Law, however, must also underscore the reality of wickedness and evil. From the time of the Fall, rebellion and disobedience have characterized the human race (Rom 3:10-20). While redemption is one aspect of justice and righteousness, so is punishment of wrongdoers (Ex 34:6-7). This has been called God's "retributive justice." God abhors evil, and he enjoined his people to abhor it as well (Lev 19:2).[4]

Punishment, then, served to purge the community of evil (Deut 13:1-5) and deter others from disobedience (Deut 13:6-11; Ps 76:8-10). Yet even God's rebuke was designed to bring about the redemption of the wrongdoer.[5] This is nowhere more plain than in God's treatment of Israel. For their disobedience he sent them into exile. But this punishment was also his effort to woo them back to himself (cf. Jer 29:10-14).

This redemptive purpose of punishment was acknowledged in the prayer of David following his adultery with Bathsheba and murder of Uriah. David cried out: "Save me from bloodguilt, O God, the God who saves me, and my tongue will sing of your righteousness" (Ps 51:14). What David was asking for cannot be justice in the sense of vindication, since he was the wrongdoer (as he has confessed freely in verses 1-5). So why did David offer to sing of God's righteousness? Because he recognized that God will redeem the penitent wrongdoer, *and that this is a characteristic of righteousness.*[6]

The Terminology of Justice
For a generation, law students taking criminal law courses have focused almost exclusively on procedural issues. What does the constitution require for a prosecution to proceed *fairly*, from arrest to trial and punishment? For most lawyers (and many Americans) justice has come to mean *due process* of law.

There are historical reasons for this development, as we have seen. Due process or fairness is certainly an important dimension of justice, particularly given the powers of the state in prosecuting defendants. But biblical justice means far more than due process. It is also more than fulfilling God's prescribed judgments to purge the community of evil. It also incorporates notions of righteousness, peace and love. Perhaps we should begin by looking at two Hebrew words which are rich in meaning and are worth remembering as we discuss criminal justice.[7]

The first word appears in two forms: *tsedeq* and *tsedaqah,* and is translated "righteous" or "just." These words were derived from the word meaning "straight" in a physical sense,[8] and eventually came to mean conformity to a standard. For example, Moses insisted that weights and measures be *tsedeq* or just (Lev 19:36). The familiar words from the twenty-third psalm assure us that the Lord leads us along *tsedeq* paths—walkable paths, or paths of righteousness. Something which meets its standard, then, is *tsedeq*. It is just, or righteous.

Tsedeq thus became a legal term, meaning the abstract standard of behavior that humans are to conform to in their relationships with each other and with God.[9] Moses instructs the people to appoint judges who will judge fairly. "Follow justice *[tsedaqah]* and justice alone" (Deut 16:20). Abraham believed God, and we are told that God counted that faithfulness as righteousness *[tsedaqah]* (Gen 15:6).

The second word is *mishpat* which means "justice" in the judicial sense. It refers to the judgments in which rights and responsibilities are determined and enforced in a legal proceeding (1 Kings 20:40). So it refers to the laws themselves (the Book of the Covenant—Exodus 21—23—is called the *mishpatim* in Hebrew).[10] *Mishpat* also refers to the legal rights that an individual may enforce in court (Is 5:7).

Mishpat, then, can refer to the formal process of applying *tsedaqah* to a particular legal dispute. It is the legal means by which the community determined whether or not the standard of justice had been violated.

The interplay of these two words is brought out by Isaiah in a clever but horrifying play on words:

And he looked for justice *[mishpat]*,
   but saw bloodshed *[mishpah]*,
for righteousness *[tsedaqah]*,
   but heard cries of distress *[tseaqah]*. (Is 5:7)[11]

Throughout Scripture, another word commonly linked with justice and righteousness is *hesed*, often translated "love," and frequently found in parallel with *righteousness* or *justice*.

Righteousness and justice are the foundation of your throne;
   love and faithfulness go before you. (Ps 89:14)

I will sing of your love and justice;
   to you, O LORD, I will sing praise. (Ps 101:1)

Continue your love to those who know you,
your righteousness to the upright in heart. (Ps 36:10)

Sow for yourselves righteousness,
reap the fruit of unfailing love. (Hos 10:12)

I will betroth you to me forever;
I will betroth you in righteousness and justice,
in love and compassion.
I will betroth you in faithfulness,
and you will acknowledge the LORD. (Hos 2:19-20)

There are several Hebrew words which we translate "love." The one used in these passages is *hesed*. However,

"Love" is a misleading translation because it *[hesed]* is always a matter of intention, having regard to what is just, and not a spontaneous, personal feeling. . . . Love may, or may not, find expression in *hesed*, which is always governed by objective considerations. A better translation, though not quite adequate, is "loyalty."[12]

David brings out this understanding of faithful, loyal, justice-oriented love:

One thing God has spoken,
two things have I heard:
that you, O God, are strong,
and that you, O LORD, are loving *[hesed]*.
Surely you will reward each person
according to what he has done. (Ps 62:11-12)

But *hesed* is not simply a characteristic of God. It is also an expected dimension of relationships between humans, as the prophet Micah makes clear:

He has showed you, O man, what is good.
And what does the LORD require of you?
To act justly and to love mercy *[hesed]*

and to walk humbly with your God. (6:8)

And finally, there is the word *shalom*. This wonderful word means completeness, fulfillment, wholeness—restored relationship.[13] It is the relationship that God desires to enjoy with his people, and to have them experience with each other. According to Isaiah, justice and righteousness are the cause of peace:

Justice will dwell in the desert
    and righteousness live in the fertile field.
The fruit of righteousness will be peace *[shalom]*;
    the effect of righteousness will be
    quietness and confidence forever.
My people will live in peaceful *[shalom]* dwelling places,
    in secure homes,
    in undisturbed places of rest. (Is 32:16-18)

Shalom thus means more than the absence of conflict (the classic Greek meaning). It includes notions of harmony, contentment and reconciliation.[14] It is the ideal state in which the community is to function. It is not simply the absence of crime or war; it is also the security, prosperity and blessing that result from corporate righteousness.

A word derived from the same root as *shalom* is *shillum*, meaning "restitution" (Ex 21:36). Restitution was the penalty imposed on one member of the community who had wronged another: he was required to pay back the victim several times the loss. This act not only brought wholeness to the victim, but also served to restore the relationship between the victim and offender and thus restored wholeness *(shalom)* to the community.

At the risk of oversimplification, but keeping in mind the serious practical problems facing us in criminal justice, I hazard this conclusion: *Shalom* (peace) is a result of *tsedeqah* (the justice of righteous living) that *mishpat* (the justice system) should uphold. We are called to demonstrate our *hesed* (steadfast, loyal love) to God and to those around us by seeing that our communities exhibit *shalom*, our lives demonstrate *tsedeqah,* and that *mishpat* promotes peace and righteousness.

Justice is far more than fair treatment and due process. It is also more than vindication of those who have been wronged and punishment of the wrongdoer. The full meaning of justice is to establish once again the *shalom* that existed before the offense. Justice is active and relational and it is redemptive in its intent.

Justice and the Law

God is the source of justice in the biblical view. He has revealed his just and righteous character in his acts, in the Law which he gave to the people of Israel and in his judgments. The Law governed not only the relationship of Israel to him, but also the way that citizens of Israel were to treat each other and the aliens living with them.

There are several interesting things in how biblical characters responded to the Law. First, *everyone was subject to the law,* including the rulers. David's delight in the Law is evident in his psalms, and it is clear that he was governed by it. David, after all, was a king after God's own heart.

But it is the behavior of a reprobate king, Ahab, which perhaps illustrates this best (1 Kings 21).[15] Ahab is described as having done more evil in the eye of the Lord than any of his predecessors. In fact, he married the daughter of a neighboring king and began serving Baal, the god of his wife's people.

Ahab wanted the property of a neighbor named Naboth. The land had been held by Naboth's ancestors, but it was adjacent to the palace and Ahab wanted to use it as a vegetable garden. Naboth refused to sell the land, saying, "The LORD forbid that I should give you the inheritance of my fathers" (1 Kings 21:3).

Ahab's response was to sulk. When his wife Jezebel asked what was wrong with him, and he explained to her the problem, she was surprised at him. "Is this how you act as king of Israel?" she asked.

In her country, what the king wanted, the king took. The law did not inhibit him, since the Phoenician king was considered the source of the law. In Israel this was not the case. Even the king was subject to the Law. So Jezebel arranged for the judicial execution of Naboth by having false witnesses testify against him, and after his death Ahab became the owner of his land.

As evil as Ahab was, he recognized the limitations which the Law placed on him. In Israel, even kings were to be subject to the Law.

Second, *the administration of justice was not always just.* The judges and rulers who decided cases did not always decide them justly, often accepting bribes to pervert the ends of justice. The prophets denounce this:

Woe to those who make unjust laws,
    to those who issue oppressive decrees,
to deprive the poor of their rights
    and rob my oppressed people of justice,
making widows their prey
    and robbing the fatherless. (Is 10:1-2)

The legal process, therefore, could be used to pervert justice and to bring about the very thing which the Law was meant to prevent.[16] Those who abused the Law were opposed by the prophets: "They sell the righteous for silver, and the needy for a pair of sandals" (Amos 2:6).

The New Testament teaches that even when the authorities are unjust they are to be honored. Paul wrote that Christians are to be submissive to their rulers. Government was established by God to maintain order, so those rebelling against its authority rebel against God (Rom 13:1-5). But this did not mean mindless obedience. Disobedience was required when the authorities violated the direct command of God. Peter and John, appearing before the Sanhedrin, recognized that the authorities had the power to punish them for their disobedience. They chose to obey God and accept punishment (Acts 5:29-41). The law is not the same as justice.

Further, *the Law was a teacher.* Lawrence Kohlberg, a Harvard researcher, has found that most Americans equate morality with keeping the law. The question of whether something is right or wrong is answered by checking to see whether it is illegal. If it is not, it must be right.[17] Scripture views the relationship of Law and justice differently. Certainly the Law was to be obeyed.[18] But the people understood that the Law was a teacher, a direction-setter. The point was not simply to avoid breaking it, but to live within its spirit. That was a major emphasis of Jesus' teaching in the Sermon on the Mount (Mt 5:21-48).

If the Law is a teacher, then knowledge of the Law is essential. Some of the most troubled periods in Israel's history occurred when the Law was not taught. Grave social consequences resulted, and were attributed to lack of knowledge of the Law. How can one be just or righteous when one does not know God, the source of justice and righteousness, or the Law which gives it concrete form?

The prophet Hosea, in a stinging indictment of rampant crime and injustice, blamed it on the people's lack of knowledge:

There is no faithfulness, no love,
    no acknowledgment of God in the land.
There is only cursing, lying and murder,
    stealing and adultery;
they break all bounds,
    and bloodshed follows bloodshed. . . .
My people are destroyed from lack of
    knowledge. (Hos 4:1-2, 6)

Finally, *the Law could not compel righteousness*. The source of sin and of injustice is the heart. This is reaffirmed throughout Scripture. Grieved at the sinfulness of the human race, the Lord determined to destroy all life, saving only Noah and his family and the animals with them: "The LORD saw how great man's wickedness on the earth had become, and that every inclination of the thoughts of his heart was only evil all the time" (Gen 6:5).

The psalmist writes of a treacherous friend:

My companion attacks his friends;
   he violates his covenant.
His speech is smooth as butter,
   yet war is in his heart;
his words are more soothing than oil,
   yet they are drawn swords. (Ps 55:20-21)

Jesus Christ, condemning the spiritual pride of the Pharisees, warns that it is not what goes into the stomach that makes one unclean, but what comes out of the heart:

Evil thoughts, sexual immorality, theft, murder, adultery, greed, malice, deceit, lewdness, envy, slander, arrogance and folly. All these evils come from inside and make a man "unclean." (Mk 7:21-23)

This being the case, both God's Law and human law are limited in their ability to sustain righteousness.

The state, through force, can compel the external behavior of individuals to conform to the demands of justice. But the state cannot measure or control the motivations which inform external behavior. Indeed, since the element of force or coercion is always implicit in policies of state, to compel "righteousness" would be to force love.[19]

Individuals can ignore the Law (Amos 2:6), the powerful can impose unjust laws (Jer 34), and the whole community might agree to overlook just provisions of the Law for mutual convenience (Jer 31:31-33). But there can be *shalom* only when people are both just and righteous (Jer 6:14; Is 59:8). The Law may point the direction, may give instructions, but if the people do not follow that way, it is limited in its power to restrain them. It is a fragile fence which can be crossed by a people bent on ignoring or perverting it. Law and justice are linked, but are not the same thing.

This is critical to our understanding of justice in society. Law may indeed promote order. But the order may not be just.

One of the central themes in Paul's writings was that the Law could not bring righteousness. In fact, the Law testifies against human unrighteousness. It is only through the redemption (there is that word again!) offered by Christ that we become righteous.

Jeremiah foresaw a time when the Law would be internal:

"The time is coming," declares the LORD,

"when I will make a new covenant. . . .

I will put my law in their minds

and write it on their hearts.

I will be their God,

and they will be my people." (Jer 31:31-33)

Conclusion

We have identified several key components of justice and righteousness. First, their source is the character of God himself, who demonstrates them in his redemptive acts, his Law and punishment.

We have also seen that the biblical terms for *justice* are much richer in connotation than we usually assume. Justice establishes a standard, to be sure, but it also is the means of upholding that standard. It assumes a relationship between the parties, and requires a loving commitment to see wrongs addressed and the parties reconciled. It is therefore related to *shalom*—peace as the result of doing justice.

Finally, although the Law reveals the just character of God, it is not itself justice, nor is it able to sustain justice if the people are unwilling. At its best, the Law points to justice, but it may also be perverted to serve unjust ends.

Then what specifically did the Law tell the people of Israel about "criminal" justice? What can we learn that will help us deal with the problem of crime, with victims and offenders?

Chapter 10

The Law and Criminal Justice

T*he story of* Solomon's dream is a familiar one. Relatively early in his reign, after he had consolidated his power, the Lord appeared to him at night and offered to give him whatever he wanted. Solomon confessed his insecurity at assuming the throne, particularly in administering justice. So he asked for a discerning heart to be able to rule wisely and to judge between right and wrong.

The request pleased God, since Solomon had asked for a gift which would enable him to perform the work God had given him, rather than one that would benefit him personally. So God gave Solomon wisdom in administering justice and promised him that if he followed in his father's steps and heeded the Law, he would enjoy a long life as well (1 Kings 3:5-15).

The administration of justice was part of the king's responsibility (1

Kings 3:11). As we have seen, he did not enforce laws which he had created, but acted on behalf of the Lord in enforcing the Law, the commandments laid down when the nation was formed.

It is a bit intimidating to begin reading the Law. For one thing, there are over six hundred commandments listed, and they are not all in one place.[1] (No wonder Solomon needed help!) Some of them look familiar to us, but others deal with problems or circumstances that we never encounter. For example, right after a lengthy section dealing with theft, usury, perjury and bribery, we encounter rules about the sabbath, instructions about three annual festivals during which the nation was to gather to worship the Lord, and a prohibition against cooking a young goat in its mother's milk (Ex 22:1—23:19).

So before we look at specific provisions of the Law, let's try to get our bearings. Several distinctions will help us sort through the specific provisions and focus on the parts that are especially significant for our discussion.

Theologians and Old Testament scholars have generally divided the content of the Law into three categories: moral, civil and religious. *Moral laws* are those which instructed the Israelites how to relate to others. There is, for example, a command requiring a day of rest each week: "Six days do your work, but on the seventh day do not work, so that your ox and your donkey may rest and the slave born in your household, and the alien as well, may be refreshed" (Ex 23:12). The reason given for this command is that people and animals need rest. It is not right to make them work every day, even though that may mean profits decline.

Religious laws are those that governed the way Israel was to worship the Lord. "If someone's offering is a fellowship offering, and he offers an animal from the herd, whether male or female, he is to present before the LORD an animal without defect" (Lev 3:1).

The *civil laws* are more familiar to us. These are similar to the types of laws that we deal with in legislatures or courts today: prohibitions against obstructing justice, laws against using false scales or measures, or penalties for theft.

Very neat. Unfortunately, it is not quite that neat or simple. The lines between these categories of Law are sometimes indistinct, sometimes hardly visible at all. For example, the requirement of rest on the sabbath, given as a *moral* law in Exodus 23:12, is also commanded on *religious* grounds: "Remember the Sabbath day by keeping it holy. Six days you shall labor and do all your work, but the seventh day is a Sabbath to the LORD your God. On it you shall not do any work" (Ex 20:8-11). And a command which looks to us today like a health or civil law—the prohibition against cooking young goats in their mothers' milk—was probably a religious law, since it forbade Israelites to participate in the fertility rites that other Canaanite nations followed.[2]

Israel Compared to Other Nations

Virtually everyone who has made the comparison agrees that the Old Testament Law presents a significant advance over the laws of the nations which surrounded Israel or which preceded it. Christopher Wright has characterized this advance in two phrases: Life was more important than property. People were more important than the punishment to be imposed.[3] Several examples may help us understand the significance of this change.

Life more important than property. The first example is the well-known principle of an eye for an eye and a tooth for a tooth, known as the *lex talionis* (Ex 21:23-25). This is often quoted today as a justification for revenge or retaliation. But at the time, it was understood to be a principle of proportion, a *limitation* on revenge. There was to be punishment, but it could not exceed the harm caused to the victim.[4] So in the case of a nonviolent property crime, the punishment could not be physical punishment or death. Instead, as we shall see, the offender was to pay restitution to the victim.

This was not the case in other nations. The Code of Hammurabi (around 1700 B.C.), the law governing Babylon, originally called for the death penalty in all cases of theft. Eventually this was relaxed, but the sentences remained excessively harsh.[5] For example, if a home-owner caught a burglar breaking into his house, he could have him executed and his body walled up in the hole that he had made break-ing in.[6] In contrast, the Old Testament provision on burglary required the burglar to make restitution. There was provision for self-defense if the burglary took place at night, but interestingly, if the burglary took place during the day, the homeowner was forbidden to use dead-ly force in trying to catch the burglar (Ex 22:2-3). For Israel, life was more important than property.

There is another way in which this principle was demonstrated. The murder statutes of surrounding nations treated the propertied nobility differently from commoners, slaves and women. The Laws of Eshnunna (around 1700 B.C.), a Mesopotamian law code, provided that the murderer of a free man's female slave had to pay restitution, but the murderer of a free man's wife or child would be executed.[7] The Code of Hammurabi had similar class distinctions.[8]

In contrast, there is no footnote to the sixth commandment exempt-ing nobility or restricting it to cases where the victim is a free male. The Law applied regardless of the social status of the victim or offend-er. Life was worth more than property, and offenders were not ex-cused from personal responsibility because of their (or the victims') position in the community.

People more important than punishment. The principle that persons were more important than things also influenced the kind and extent of punishment imposed. For example, Old Testament Law specifically forbade holding another person responsible for the actions of an offender. Babylonian law provided that if a free man killed the daugh-ter of another free man, it was the murderer's daughter, not the murderer, who was put to death. In contrast, the Mosaic Law provided that "fathers shall not be put to death for their children, nor children put to death for their fathers; each is to die for his own sin" (Deut 24:16). The doctrine of individual responsibility was an important development. One could not be held accountable for the actions of another over whom he had no control. The offender was responsible for his own intentional actions.

A second example of the humanitarian nature of the Old Testament Law is the provision of cities of refuge (Deut 4:41-43; 19:1-3; Num 35:6-34). Both Israel and its neighbors recognized the right of a person needing protection from revenge to go to the altar in the temple, where he was to be kept from harm until the matter could be decided through formal judicial process (Ex 21:12-14).[9] But the altar might be far away, and the wrongly accused person might be caught before reaching the protection of the sanctuary. So the Law provided for six cities of refuge, which were to be centrally located and reached by well-built roads, so that someone suspected of murder could get to protection easily.

The need for the protection stemmed from a practice that existed before the Law was given. If a person was killed, the victim's next-of-kin was expected to seek revenge. The Law recognized that this anticipated retaliation would be unjust in cases of accidental death and provided that someone who unintentionally killed another could flee to a city of refuge and argue his case to the elders of the city. If the death was found to have been accidental, then the avenger was not allowed to harm him so long as he stayed in the city until the death of the high priest.

People were more important than punishment. And as a result, procedural safeguards were built into the Law so that the rights of the offender could be protected while the case was being considered by judicial authorities.

We have talked about individual responsibility (p. 130), but there was corporate responsibility as well. The community was not responsible for the behavior of individuals in the sense that those individuals were no longer accountable for their own behavior. But the community was responsible for seeing that justice was done. The verse following the passage on individual responsibility emphasizes this:

Do not deprive the alien or the fatherless of justice, or take the cloak of the widow as a pledge. Remember that you were slaves in Egypt and the LORD your God redeemed you from there. That is why I command you to do this. (Deut 24:17-18)

The alien, the fatherless and the widow were the people least able to assert their own rights. The nation was commanded to protect the rights of those most vulnerable to losing them. This included those who had been victimized, as well as those unjustly accused of crimes.

So in at least two significant ways, the Old Testament Law was an advance over other ancient law codes. It valued life over property, and it valued people over punishment.

Old Testament Punishments
This does not mean that there was no punishment. But, as we have seen, the Law was not a "vindictive" code as some have claimed by making a false distinction between judgment in the Old Testament and grace in the New Testament. Both judgment and grace are found throughout Scripture.[10] One form of Old Testament "grace" was the requirement that punishment serve to restore.

There were basically three forms of punishment for people who had violated the civil portions of the Law: execution, corporal punishment and restitution. *Death* was prescribed for murder, kidnaping, some sexual offenses such as adultery or incest, and for deliberately subverting the judicial process (in addition to various forms of religious and ceremonial offenses).[11] (We will discuss capital punishment further in chapter 13.)

Corporal punishment was apparently rarely practiced. Mutilation is provided for in only one instance (Deut 25:11-12), a very unlikely one at that. (One would, incidentally, expect mutilation to be more common if the *lex talionis* were viewed as setting out the specific punishment to be imposed, instead of being seen as the upper limit on punishment as we discussed earlier.)

Beating was the other form of corporal punishment. While the Old Testament contains no specific laws calling for beating as a punishment, a provision outlining how court proceedings were to be governed specified that someone found deserving of a beating was to be flogged in the presence of the judge with the number of lashes his crime deserved. In any event, he was not to receive more than forty lashes, for "if he is flogged more than that, your brother will be degraded in your eyes" (Deut 25:1-3).

By far the most frequent punishment was restitution. The victim was to be paid back. Before looking at this in greater detail, let us note that *two forms of modern punishment are conspicuous by their absence from the Law: imprisonment and fines.*

As we have seen earlier, *imprisonment* as a form of punishment is a recent invention. The prisons we read about in Scripture were simply used to hold persons accused of crime or other offenses until the case was decided and the punishment selected (Lev 24:12). Even Joseph's imprisonment in Egypt, as the story of his fellow prisoners the butler and the cook shows, was only for the purpose of holding him until the Pharaoh remembered he was there and decided to make a judgment on the case (Gen 39—40).[12] Israel did not use prisons at all.

Fines are not mentioned either. Compensation was to be made to the victim, not to the state.

Restitution in Scripture

The kinds of offenses which resulted in restitution sanctions included both property offenses (such as theft) and violent crimes (such as battery). Most of Exodus 21—22 is devoted to various cases of restitution. Let's look at several examples in detail:

1. *Battery (even with a deadly weapon).*

If men quarrel and one hits the other with a stone or with his fist and he does not die but is confined to bed, the one who struck the blow will not be held responsible if the other gets up and walks around outside with his staff; however, he must pay the injured man for the loss of his time and see that he is completely healed. (Ex 21:18-19)

2. Theft of property.

If a man steals an ox or a sheep and slaughters it or sells it, he must pay back five head of cattle for the ox and four sheep for the sheep. . . . If the stolen animal is found alive in his possession—whether ox or donkey or sheep—he must pay back double. (Ex 22:1, 4)

3. Illegal possession of stolen property.

If a man gives his neighbor silver or goods for safekeeping and they are stolen from the neighbor's house, the thief, if he is caught, must pay back double. But if the thief is not found, the owner of the house must appear before the judges to determine whether he has laid his hands on the other man's property. In all cases of illegal possession of an ox, a donkey, a sheep, a garment, or any other lost property about which somebody says, "This is mine," both parties are to bring their cases before the judges. The one whom the judges declare guilty must pay back double to his neighbor. (Ex 22:7-9)

There were also provisions concerning damage done through negligence. These too provided for restitution (Ex 22:5-6, 10-13, 14-15). Notice that the amount of restitution varies. In some cases the offender paid back double, in others as much as four or five times the amount of the victim's loss. The question of how much restitution should be required is discussed in Appendix B. For our purposes now, it is sufficient to note that having to pay the victim back was the dominant punishment in the Old Testament Law.

Restitution continued to be the principal punishment for the people of Israel throughout Scripture. We read of the prophet Nathan coming before David after the king had committed adultery with Bathsheba and murdered Uriah. Nathan tells David of the "case" of a wealthy landowner who had stolen the only lamb of a poor man in order to feed a guest. Although David was furious, saying that a man like that deserved to die, he decreed that the rich man pay the poor man four sheep (2 Sam 12:1-14; cf. Ex 22:1-2). Of course, he then learned that the "case" had been a parable, and that he himself was the greedy and guilty man.

The New Testament provides us with the case of Zacchaeus, the dishonest tax collector. After his confrontation with Jesus, he repented and promised to pay back fourfold anyone he had cheated (Lk 19:1-10). It should not surprise us, then, that the Christian church has historically emphasized the need for restitution.[13]

Restitution and the Purposes of Punishment

In chapter 7 we discussed the changing views of the purpose of punishment. How does restitution relate to these purposes?

Retribution requires responsibility, a responsibility primarily to the victim, and only secondarily to the state. Human dignity is preserved when the free will of the offender is recognized and when the offense is understood as an injury to another person.

Restitution, then, clearly meets the minimum requirement of retribution. But it has the advantage of restoring the victim, consistent with the emphasis of Scripture. In his anger, David exclaimed that the rich man who had stolen the poor man's only sheep deserved to die. That is the revenge that David wanted to take. But the Law required only that the victim be restored fourfold (Ex 22:1-2). And this would be a great deal more meaningful to the poor man than the rich man's death.

Rehabilitation is the principle that punishment should change the offender. Some have argued that this is a characteristic of restitution, since it requires offenders to understand the real consequences of their actions, and gives them a way to deal directly with those consequences. Psychologist Albert Eglash, for example, maintains that "restitution is something an inmate does, not something done for or to him. . . . Being reparative, restitution can alleviate guilt and anxiety, which can otherwise precipitate further offenses.[14] (We will explore the effect of restitution on offenders in chapter 12.) But rehabilitation of the offender must be viewed as a corollary benefit, not as the governing principle of restitution. The principal purpose of restitution is to restore *shalom:* to punish offenders by requiring them to repay their victims. The means of doing that may very well have rehabilitative consequences, but that is not the key.

Furthermore, we could argue that rehabilitation turns the criminal justice system on its head. It says that the responsibility of the system is to "restore" the offender, rather than to see that the offender restores the victim.

This is not to say that rehabilitation programs are worthless. They should be offered to offenders who could benefit from them. But offenders should not be given a particular sentence because of its rehabilitative potential alone. *They should be sentenced to restore the victims.*

With respect to *deterrence,* virtually any sanction, imposed swiftly and surely, has a deterrent effect. An effectively run restitution program, therefore, will deter.

But justice, in the biblical view, is not primarily a calculation of the amount of pain needed to deter others from the pleasure of criminal activity. It addresses the harm caused to the victim and surrounding community and emphasizes restoration of the victim and the broken *shalom.*

And what if the offender cannot pay the victim? The Old Testament Law provided that a person unable to pay restitution be sold as a slave to pay for the loss (Ex 22:3). If this sounds strange, remember that slavery in the Old Testament was a temporary condition. Insolvent debtors were forced to work off their debt for a maximum of six years, and at the end of the time received sufficient payment to make a new start (Ex 21:2-6; Deut 15:12-18).

While slavery *per se* is not an option today, the principle still holds: offenders should have to work off their debts if they cannot pay. This could be done by requiring offenders to work and devote a specified amount of their pay to restitution. Or they could be ordered to perform services for the victims or the community in return for state-paid compensation. (We will discuss the possibilities of community service restitution in chapter 12.)

Incapacitation prevents offenders from committing new crimes while being punished. Restitution does not directly address this. Even offenders who are conscientiously repaying their victims may commit other crimes. In fact, they may be tempted to commit new crimes in order to make the restitution payments. Supervision of offenders is important. But there are methods short of imprisonment, such as halfway houses, intensive supervision and house arrest, that can provide appropriate incapacitation for many of the people who need it.

Reconciliation

We noted in the last chapter that one of the characteristics of justice in the Old Testament is that it promotes reconciliation. The standard *[tsedaqah]* that is sought is *shalom*. A key underlying purpose of the Law was to guide the community into *shalom*. When the peace had been broken, the Law prescribed how to right the wrong and restore *shalom* to the community.

Clearly we cannot hang too much on the criminal justice system. Injustice anywhere in society ruptures *shalom*. For example, we cannot talk about biblical justice without noting that on many occasions it refers to fair treatment of the poor in society (see Deut 10:18; Ps 82:3-4; Amos 2:7; Jer 22:3-4). Simply moving to restitution in our *criminal* cases will neither bring about a just society nor guarantee *shalom*. But it is a move in the right direction and can help heal the wounds of crime and punishment in our country today.

Reconciliation is more than simply restoring the financial loss of the victim. There is a broken relationship which must be restored as well. The Old Testament recognized that this relationship did not end when the crime ended. In fact, the punishment was mitigated because of this relationship: the injunction against beating a convicted offender more than forty times referred to him as "your brother" (Deut 25:3).

Victims are my sisters and brothers, but so are offenders. My responsibility is to see that the injuries are repaired and relationships restored.

Is this "utopian"? I'd rather call it "visionary." We need a new vision in criminal justice, something that enables us to approach the many practical dilemmas of crime and punishment with both realism and hope.

Conclusion

We have been on a journey into biblical times, exploring how Scripture deals with the problem of crime and criminal justice. What have we learned that can help us respond to the problems we face today?

First of all, the purpose of justice is a healthy community. This means more than simply a place where people live near each other. It is characterized by *shalom*, by an active, creative, reconciling peace. There will be conflicts in the community, and people will hurt others. These conflicts and injuries can destroy *shalom* and result in neighborhoods where people draw their shades, lock their doors and look after themselves. Or the conflicts can be resolved. Justice works for resolution.

Second, crime is seen principally as the injury an offender has caused to a victim. Crime certainly threatens *shalom*, but it is first and foremost an injury to the victim.

Third, law is limited in its ability to bring *shalom*, social well-being and cohesion. At its best, the law reinforces values and gives signficant ways that those values can be demonstrated. But it cannot by itself guarantee that members of the community will uphold it. Two implications must be noted. First, there will always be some crime. Second, and more important, we must form our community around values that we agree on, and which we agree to reinforce through our families, our institutions and the criminal justice system.

Finally, the objective of the criminal justice system must be to help restore community by resolving the injury that the offender has caused the victim. Offenders are to be held responsible for restoring the victim. And the relationship between the victim and the offender is to be restored. Both are to be reintegrated into the community. The offender should be removed only if there is no other option.

A criminal justice system based on restitution deals with the victim, the offender and the community. It restores the victim, holds the offender responsible, and promotes reconciliation in the community.

In the next few chapters we will look at ways in which restitution-based justice can be seen in our nation today. We need to underscore and support the ways in which our criminal justice system is already effective. We must also work to change the processes and punishments which prevent us from reaching our goal of a healthy community.

In chapter 11 we will look at some of the components of a peaceful community. What can we do to actually reduce the amount of crime?

Chapter 12 explores ways that society can respond to crimes when they do occur. We will look at innovations in sentencing which are helping restore victims while holding offenders responsible.

In chapter 13 we will consider what to do when offenders must be restrained for the protection of society. We will look at the appropriate use of prisons and explore the ultimate restraint that we can impose on offenders: capital punishment.

Part IV

Hope for the Future

Chapter 11

Reducing Crime

W*hile I have* been discussing victims and criminals, you may have been waiting patiently (or impatiently) for me to say something about reducing crime. Dealing appropriately with victims and offenders should help do that, but there are other steps we can take to prevent crime.

Crime, the State, and Individual Responsibility
First, and perhaps most importantly, we must move away from the notion that crime is only an offense against the state. As we have seen, this is an historical and political development resulting from conflict between himself and his barons in the Middle Ages. The king defined injuries against citizens as an injury to himself so that he could gain control over the judicial process and benefit financially from the fines

imposed on guilty defendants.[1]

King Henry had found a way to *compel* parties to bring their cases to his court: by defining those offenses first and foremost as crimes against the state. We have seen the effect on victims, who have become simply a part of the state's case, and on offenders who are forced to accept responsibility for the "injury" they have done to the state, but not for the injury they have done to other people.

This development may actually contribute to the problem of crime by reinforcing the ways in which offenders rationalize their criminal behavior. One study has categorized typical rationalizations into five major groups:

1. Denial of responsibility. Offenders treat the crime as an accident, or blame their actions on factors out of their control—their upbringing, how they are treated in the community, and so forth.

2. Denial of injury. Offenders question whether anyone was really hurt, viewing theft as borrowing, or seeing fights as private matters that do not concern the community.

3. Denial of victim. Offenders conclude that no "real" victim was harmed by what they did. They were either retaliating for something done to them, or the victim—say, a homosexual, drunkard, cheat or member of a discredited political group—was not entitled to protection.

4. Condemnation of the condemners. Offenders focus on the unfairness or hypocrisy of the accusers, the courts or the police, and thereby alleviate their own responsibility.

5. Appeal to higher loyalties. Offenders argue that they violated the rights of others and the law in order to protect the interests of friends or groups to which they owed allegiance.[2]

I suggest that these denials are reinforced by our criminal justice system which, until recently at least, has held that offenders have limited responsibility, treated the injuries as an abstract "wrong" done to the state, denied that there are personal victims whose interests must be protected, and claimed loyalty solely by force. In other words, each of the denials is supported, not dispelled, by the criminal justice system.

So a starting point for reducing crime is to agree to view it primarily as an offense against other people. Victims and offenders are the key players, and the state's principal role should be to represent the community's interest in seeing that the offense is resolved appropriately. We must object to the view that crime is simply an injury to the monarch or to the state. It is fundamentally an injury to a victim and should be treated accordingly.

Character and Crime

If crime is a dimension of individual responsibility, why have some periods of our country's history been more crime-filled than others? This is a question raised by criminologist James Q. Wilson and psychologist Richard J. Herrnstein in a fascinating and groundbreaking new book *Crime and Human Nature.*

Wilson and Herrnstein suggest that these differences in crime rates can be explained by three factors: first, changes in the population that increase or decrease the proportion of people who are constitutionally disposed to crime; second, changes in the benefits versus the costs of criminal behavior; and third, changes in the amount of societal investment in character development. They define character development as "inculcating an internalized commitment to self-control" as opposed to self-expression.[3]

Wilson and Herrnstein draw some surprising conclusions about which of the three has been most important in affecting crime rates in the last one hundred fifty years. Using a number of relatively recent studies on crime rates in America and Europe, they discount the significance of family life, urbanization, and the number of people in the crime-prone years (fifteen to twenty-five). While those and other conditions may contribute, they do not offer satisfying explanations for those times when crime declined.

What may provide such an explanation is the amount of *investment in character* during different periods. They note that the decline in crime rates which began in the midnineteenth century and continued into the early part of this century took place at a time of great social upheaval: the Civil War and the industrial revolution that led to increased numbers of people living in large metropolitan areas, as well as to children leaving their families much earlier than they do today. They contrast that with the steady rise in crime rates in this century (which, of course, has also experienced social upheaval).

A series of reform movements swept across America beginning in the 1820s and 1830s. The Second Great Awakening, the Sunday-school movement, the development of the YMCA and YWCA and other institutions which provided homes and education for young people immigrating to the cities for work, and the temperance movement were examples of a wide effort to either enhance the role of families in building character, or to supply substitutes for those familial influences during a time of growing personal liberty and rapid social change. The goal was to create in individuals "self-control and thereby enhance character."[4]

In the 1920s this began to change. Wilson and Herrnstein describe this as the move from self-restraint to self-expression.[5] Freedom of choice, rather than the need for inner control, began to be emphasized. One-third of the child-raising articles in the *Ladies Home Journal, Woman's Home Companion* and *Good Housekeeping* in 1890, 1900 and 1910 discussed character development, whereas in 1920 only three per cent did. And by 1930, articles on moral character were absent, replaced with articles on personality development.[6] The Depression, the Second World War and the small population of males in the crime-prone ages helped depress the crime rates until the baby boom came of age in the 1960s and 1970s, and crime rates started to rise. "Self-expression" had come home to roost.

Can crime be related to national values? National values are a composite of personal values. As we saw in chapter 9, Scripture attributes the failure of families and priests to adequately teach the Law, and the failure of the people to obey it, for the rampant crime and social injustice that marked phases of Israel's history. Crime comes from the heart (Ps 55:20-21; Mk 7:21-23).

Others have agreed. Dr. Robert Coles, a psychiatrist who teaches at Harvard, has pointed out that when children raise ethical questions, they are often viewed as symptoms of a psychological problem, not as questions which deserve answers. At one psychiatric conference a child who had seen television reports of starvation in Africa and had then questioned his parents about their clothing, jewelry and vacations was described as "hostile" and "passive-aggressive." Coles agrees that it is helpful to consider motives, but wonders why the child wasn't helped in drawing moral connections between the way his parents lived and the way others live.

> The longer I do my work with children and their parents here and abroad, the more I come to realize how prominently a covert kind of moral instruction figures in family life—even though, ironically, for all our attention to children these days, in America, we have tended to neglect the moral aspect of their growth and development in favor of an emphasis on the emotional, and on the various psychological conflicts boys and girls have to confront.[7]

Community Prevention of Crime

Our country began to see a rise in crime rates starting in the 1960s. During this same time, Japan's crime rates dropped. They experienced a twenty per cent decline in total crime from 1962 to 1972. And when theft (a nonviolent offense) is excluded, there was a drop of forty per cent.[8] Observers concluded that it was the community spirit that exists among the Japanese people (who face urban crowding that makes ours look tame) that was the most important ingredient.

The Japanese people have achieved a balance between freedom and control that not only suits them but that also permits the country to grow, industrialize, and urbanize without the worst disruptions of crime. The West is looking for community crime prevention, but it does not have the required community.[9]

We can see this same phenomenon in parts of the United States. A number of communities have begun to organize in response to concern over crime. Most of us have heard of crime watch programs, or identification operations where people mark their possessions in order to reduce the opportunity for burglars to fence them. What may surprise us is how well neighborhood organizing works to reduce crime.

Detroit conducted a two-year project which involved more than 150,000 residents in voluntary neighborhood watch programs. They found that the program reduced burglaries sixty-two per cent. Overall crime went down fifty-five per cent in the targeted study area.

Seattle has one of the earliest neighborhood watch programs, the Seattle Block Watch, which started in 1973. It was so successful that the U.S. Justice Department gave it an exemplary award in 1977 after a forty-nine to sixty-one per cent drop in burglaries in the targeted neighborhoods. Since then crime has continued to drop faster in these areas than in other parts of the city.

San Diego's Community Alert program involved thirty-five per cent of the city's residents in 1983. There is good reason for others to become involved. According to the police department, most thefts and burglaries in the city happen outside of the Community Alert areas.[10]

There are now over 19,000 community crime prevention programs like these in the United States.[11] They generally focus on crimes such as burglary, theft and purse-snatching which are the most common crimes in urban neighborhoods and also the ones that are most affected by taking preventive measures.[12]

But there seems to be an additional benefit to neighborhood watch programs. Neighbors who have not known each other, and who have not worked with each other on any common projects discover that together they can help create the kind of community they want to live in. The Eisenhower Foundation in Washington, D.C., is funding a four-year study in ten urban neighborhoods to document the ability of these programs to reduce both crime and the fear of crime. But they are also studying the positive secondary benefits of neighbors talking to one another and therefore working together to solve other community problems.[13]

A Justice Department publication includes this dimension in its definition of neighborhood watch programs:

Neighborhood crime prevention is people taking responsibility for themselves, their neighbors, and their community. It is the police and the community working together to make it harder for crime to occur. In urban areas, it is the creation or re-creation of a community atmosphere in which neighbors know neighbors and police officers know the community. It is people helping each other make a better place in which to live.[14]

Interestingly, participants in neighborhood watch programs appear to have more faith in the criminal justice system than nonparticipants and are much less likely to rely on traditional "get tough" solutions to the crime problem.[15]

Other studies have documented the importance of joining together with others nearby in reducing the fear of crime. In fact, living alone is a strong predictor of fear of crime, as is the sense that no one is watching or that no one would intervene in a risky situation. Holding meetings, contacting neighbors door-to-door and publicizing the program increases the sense that neighbors are supportive, and reduces fear.[16]

In regard to developing a sense of community, block associations have been one of the most effective ways of bringing people together. In city after city, the majority of block members report that they had never known most of their neighbors and that only through the block club coffee sessions and regular meetings and the door-to-door contact had they really gotten to know each other and to appreciate mutual problems. . . . Crime prevention provided the motivation to get together, and block associations offered the mechanism for doing it. The simple factor of adults and youth knowing each other has helped to reduce fear. Familiarity has developed friendly attitudes and an increased concern for one's neighborhood.[17]

One study hypothesized that organizing the community around crime prevention helps establish community norms against crime and that these "contribute to a climate in which criminal actions are viewed by community youths as both risky and unacceptable rather than as a routine part of growing up."[18]

We saw earlier that one of the rationalizations of delinquents was the appeal to higher loyalties. If young people see that their parents are not interested in the people living around them, then their own loyalty to the community will be minimal. But if the parents demonstrate a high degree of concern for their neighborhood, then the competing loyalties will have to be that much stronger to justify ripping neighbors off.

In short, citizen-organizing against crime is an effective way of establishing that it is wrong to hurt others. When this is supplemented by effective police and court action, it reduces both crime and the fear of crime. Fighting crime, then, has become an opportunity for the community to say collectively that right and wrong matter. And that is important. As Lewis Smedes has written,

> It is a truism today that we are in a crisis of morals. The crisis is not simply that people are doing wrong things; that has been going on since the Fall in Eden. The crisis is the loss of a shared understanding of what is right. Worse, it is a crisis of doubt as to whether there even is a moral right or wrong at all.[19]

Values Are the Key

Religion has been the source of our values. For most Americans, Judeo-Christian teaching is the foundation of our understanding of right and wrong. This is critical in grasping ways we can reduce crime.

If there is no right or wrong, then our laws are simply arbitrary decrees passed by majority vote in a legislature and reviewed for constitutionality by the courts. We saw in chapter 9 that this is a weight the law cannot bear. God himself promised a new covenant in which the Law would be inscribed in the heart, not on mere stone. If our restraints are not found there, statutory laws will have to become incredibly complex and police forces much more powerful. Even then we will be troubled by crime.

How can we increase the importance of values? How can we ensure that common values are reinforced throughout society? One way is to strengthen the institutions in society which encourage the development of those values: the church, the family and the schools.

The church. Involvement in organized religion has been shown to reduce criminal activity. Dr. David Larson, research psychiatrist at the National Institute of Mental Health, has studied the effect of religious involvement on mental and physical health and has reviewed studies on the impact of religious commitment on delinquency. He has found surprising evidence that religious commitment, as measured by church attendance, has shown benefits in reducing both disease and delinquency.[20]

A remarkable study compared FBI crime rate data for metropolitan areas with a national, privately funded census of the proportions of church members to nonmembers in those same metropolitan areas. The study showed that the church membership rate was more significant than any of the standard variables traditionally used in such studies (unemployment rates, income levels, and so on). The researchers concluded:

> Cities with higher proportions of church members have lower rates of crime than do more secular cities. Indeed, low church membership rates help explain a very marked regional difference in crime rates. Although it has received remarkably little public notice, the Pacific region has a substantially higher total crime rate than do other parts of the nation. And the Pacific region has by far the lowest church membership rates. Those who would celebrate the low church membership in California, Oregon, Washington, Alas-

ka and Hawaii as indicative of enlightenment and as a portent of the future must also recognize the probability that this must be paid for in terms of high crime rates.[21]

Another study explored whether males affiliated with the Catholic Church, with its clear teaching on sexual morality, had a lower incidence of rape. Using control groups to test other possible explanations, the study found that the religious factor was the one most closely associated with the variance in the incidence of rape. The next highest variable was alcoholism.[22]

A study of delinquency found that boys with no religious preference committed twice as many crimes per thousand as those who had a religious preference.[23] Knowledge of the parents' religious beliefs, agreement with those beliefs, and the frequency of discussion with parents concerning them have been shown to be significantly associated with reduced delinquency.[24]

The overall effect of religious involvement on criminal behavior appears to be related to the role of "religiousness" in the community at large. A report issued by the Center for Law and Justice of the University of Washington concluded that:

> In communities where religiousness is the norm, variations in individual religiousness do have a substantial effect on delinquency. However, in highly secularized communities religion is unable to restrain the behavior of even its firm adherents.[25]

Alcoholism, drug addiction and family breakdown have been associated with criminal activity. Studies done by Larson and others have shown that narcotic addicts' and alcoholics' fathers were less involved in religious activities than were the fathers of the control group of nonaddicts,[26] that alcoholics were less involved in religious activities than the control group, that the early religious life of alcoholics tended to have created conflicts within them leading to religious confusion rather than commitment,[27] and that strong marriages were characterized by religious commitment of at least one of the partners and most strongly with commitment by both partners.[28]

The family. Values are important. They help govern our behavior. The key place for learning values (including religious values) is the family, and most people who do not commit crimes attribute their lawful behavior to their upbringing. That's what Joseph Rogers discovered when he researched and wrote *Why Are You Not a Criminal?* He reversed the question we usually ask in order to find out the range of reasons people give in accounting for their law-abiding behavior. He found that his samples referred to the family more than any other single category. Three out of five credited their family relationships and upbringing as significant factors in choosing not to commit crimes. He quotes the testimony of Dr. Robert Coles before the U.S. Senate Subcommittee on Children and Youth in 1974:

> If the family is anything, it is the medium through which one generation teaches an ethical system of values to another generation. That is what the family is all about. It is concerned with the ethical rearing of children.[29]

This is certainly a biblical understanding of the family. When God called Abraham he told him to direct his household and his descendants to do what was just and right (Gen 18:19). He later removed Eli's descendants as judges over Israel because he had not restrained his sons from doing what was evil (1 Sam 3:11-17). Proverbs gives us the familiar instruction to "train children in the way they should go" so that when they are grown they will have this ethical instruction to direct them (Prov 22:6). Paul, writing to his apprentice Timothy, reminds him of the godly faith which his grandmother and mother had instilled in him (2 Tim 1:5).

So it should not surprise us to discover that the family is key in the formation of values.

The school. A third institution in which values can be taught is the school. In recent years, there has been an attempt to develop "value-neutral" educational materials for our schools in order to respect the cultural and religious plurality of our nation. But increasingly it appears that we have gone further than necessary.

The American Institute for Character Education has developed a Character Education Curriculum based on a study of value systems throughout the world. They identified fifteen basic values which are shared by the major religions and cultures: courage, conviction, generosity, kindness, helpfulness, honesty, honor, justice, tolerance, the sound use of time and talents, freedom of choice, freedom of speech, good citizenship, the right to be an individual, and the right to equal opportunity.[30]

The curriculum has been in use in an elementary school in an economically depressed area of Indianapolis since 1970. The principal, Beatrice Bowles, described it then as looking like a school in a riot area: windows had been broken and replaced with masonite. The community viewed the school as having "gone to the dogs." The students were rude, discourteous, insolent to their teachers, and disgruntled that they had to go to "that old school."

The principal asked that the broken windows be replaced with glass and was told that this was impossible. In the last school year $3500 worth of glass had been broken, and the school district simply could not afford to make that kind of investment on a yearly basis.

That year the school began using the Character Education Program. In one year the change was noticeable. There had been less than $100 of glass broken, and most of that was accidental. Students' attitudes improved. Bowles described their mood as "respectful and cooperative with the teachers, and there is the feeling of one for all and all for one."

Five years later, Bowles reported that the program continued to be successful. "There is a noticeable improvement in the attitudes, behavior, and achievement of our children, now sixth graders, who have been in the program the entire six years. School attendance is compulsory; church attendance is not, so to my staff and me Character Education is a *must* in our school."

She also noted that as a result, teacher turnover was minimal. One substitute teacher told her that she would rather teach in her school than in any other in Indianapolis. Of course, there were other changes in those six years which may have contributed to the improved conduct, but the principal credited the course as the significant factor.[31]

The Thomas Jefferson Research Center has studied this issue for over twenty years.[32] One of the results of its research is a growing body of evidence that character education in schools is not only possible in a pluralistic society, but also can be effective in reducing lawless behavior. They have distributed the Character Education Curriculum to over 9,000 classrooms in thirty-one states.[33]

If values are key in preventing people from committing crimes, they are also the key to forming communities where crime is minimal. Perhaps the most important value is justice.

The Larger Picture: Justice

Holding offenders responsible by restoring victims is certainly not the only value in Scripture. There are others which are as important to the kind of peaceful community we desire. We have already noted that a key dimension of the biblical understanding of justice is how the poor and weak are treated. Some have argued that the poor should have reduced responsibility, or that the rich should have greater responsibility, for their criminal actions. This is not the Scriptural view. Each person is responsible for his or her own actions, and neither the rich nor the poor is to have an unfair advantage in court proceedings (Deut 16:19; Lev 19:15).

But it is clear that the community does have a responsibility to respond to the needs of the poor, particularly to help them overcome their poverty. And it is important to remember that in all countries, it is the poor who become the marginal people, the people with no power. As a result, criminal laws are passed which weigh most heavily on the poor. Anatole France said that the law "in its majestic equality forbids the rich as well as the poor to sleep under bridges, to beg in streets, and to steal bread."[34]

I thought of this when I was reading in the *Gulag Archipelago* by Aleksandr Solzhenitsyn of the lengthy prison sentences that Soviet children received for stealing when they were hungry.

And the hungry fourteen-year-old girl Lida . . . walked down the street picking up, mixed with the dust, a narrow trail of grain spilled from a truck (doomed to go to waste in any case). For this she was sentenced to only *three* years because of the alleviating circumstances that she had not taken socialist property directly from the field or from the barn.[35]

How different from the Old Testament injunction that owners of a field not harvest it twice in order to get the last pieces of grain! They were to allow the poor to glean what remained in order to live (Lev 19:9-10). The self-restraint which values bring must restrain *us*, not just the "other" people out there who threaten us. We may lose some personal advantages, but we gain more if what we are able to achieve is a healthy community, *shalom*.

Paul reminds us of this in the context of the church. He tells us to defer to one another when the issue that divides us is one that reasonable people could differ on. We should each have our own point of view, but we must allow others to have their's as well. Insisting on our own rights could hurt others, and when others are injured, it affects the righteousness, peace and joy in the Holy Spirit which should characterize the kingdom of God (Rom 14:13-18).

Justice is made of whole cloth.

Chapter 12

Responding to Crime

What should we do when our efforts to prevent crime have not worked? How can we deal with people who break the law?

Our prisons are full and overflowing. Our efforts to reduce crime by locking up criminals appear doomed to failure. We pay more and more each year for a prison system which seems to have less and less effect on crime. It is time to move back to the old notions of responsibility and restoration. The key purpose of the criminal justice system should be to hold offenders responsible to restore victims. And while this would be a revolution in criminal justice thinking, there are a number of programs already operating successfully which help us glimpse how this could be done. Here are some directions that we should pursue in accomplishing a revolution in criminal justice.

Restitution

It was only his sixth month as a trial court judge, but Judge Albert Kramer knew he had heard just about every variation on the typical defendant's plea at sentencing: give me a second chance.[1] Lawyers for disadvantaged offenders would argue "Your honor, my client comes from a split home, his father is an alcoholic, he had it bad but he promises to be good." Lawyers for privileged offenders tried the opposite approach: "Your honor, she comes from a fine family. I know them well, and I can assure you she won't do it again."

One day, out of frustration, he asked, "But who will pay the victim?" And when the lawyer replied that the parents would be happy to do so, Kramer objected. "The *parents* didn't do it. What will the *offender* do?"

When the lawyer explained that he did not have a job, Kramer vowed to get a local businessman to employ him long enough to pay restitution. "No restitution, no second chance!"

That was the beginning of Earn-It, a model restitution program operating out of Quincy, Massachusetts. The program has won national recognition, recently being named a host site by the federal Office of Juvenile Justice and Delinquency Prevention.

The most obvious way to hold offenders responsible for the injury they have caused victims is to require them to make restitution to the victim—to pay back the fair market value of the loss. This is being done in Quincy and in a number of programs around the country.[2] The following description is based on the most successful of these programs.

A key to successful restitution programs is that the payments are clearly defined, measurable, and (without being easy) can be achieved. If the court ordering restitution does not specify the amount and the payment schedule, both the offender and the victim will be frustrated, and the order will prove unenforceable. If the order requires payments that are beyond the ability of the offender, the resulting failure is predictable.

So the first step is to determine the actual loss to the victim. Successful programs like Earn-It focus on the actual loss to the victim, and do not attempt to calculate psychological harm. While ultimately it is the judge who must make the final determination of loss, Earn-It first asks the victim and offender to attempt to agree on a reasonable figure. Studies have shown that victim and offender satisfaction with the restitution order tends to be highest when both have been involved in its negotiation.[3] We will see later how this can be done.

In addition to determining the amount of the loss, the judge must consider the defendant's ability to pay. This includes not only looking at assets and income, but also at the other demands on that income in the form of dependents, usual living costs, travel to and from work, and ability to pay in installments.

The victim's circumstances must be factored into this as well. Certain losses could be reimbursed over time. Others require prompt payment in order to avoid additional losses. Some victims are insured for the loss while others are not. The victim's needs and the offender's financial circumstances are both considerations in making the final order. That is why it is helpful to have both involved in negotiating the amount and payment schedule of restitution.

The judge could order that payments be made directly to the victims, but this requires ongoing contact between victims and offenders, which may not be appropriate, and it requires victims to initiate enforcement of the order if the payments are not made. A better approach is to have payments sent to the probation department or to the clerk of the court. The check can then be forwarded to the victim. This is similar to the way some jurisdictions handle child support payments.

Most losses in property crimes are relatively small, and restitution should not pose an insurmountable problem.[4] But what happens if an offender does not make the payments? Studies have found that this happens in approximately twenty-five per cent of the cases.[5]

There are typically two reasons for failure to make payments. The defendant is either unable or unwilling to pay. In either case, the response of the court appears to be critical to the success of the program.

With employed offenders unable to make the payments as originally ordered, the payment schedule can be modified. This may be necessary when the original order was unreasonable, or when the defendants' circumstances have changed. But what about unemployed defendants?

Judge Kramer started the Earn-It program because he was faced with defendants who could not pay restitution. He met with businessmen and succeeded in getting commitments from them to hire defendants at minimum wages to work and pay restitution. Now, unemployed defendants are referred to the Earn-It staff for placement. The jobs last as long as the restitution payments, although some businesses have then hired the defendants for permanent work.

If the defendants appear able to make the payments, however, but simply refuse to do so, then the court must enforce its order. Sometimes contacting defendants to find out why the payments were not made is enough to get them started again. Other times they must be brought into court on a probation violation petition. A number of judges have tried something that Judge Kramer calls "tourniquet sentencing." Defendants who do not comply are gradually given more severe punishments designed to get them paying. Probation may be extended and court costs added to the restitution payments. If that does not work, they may be sentenced to a series of weekends in jail. All but the first weekend are suspended pending the restitution payment due that week. In essence, defendants are given a taste of jail. Then they either make the restitution payments or spend the remaining weekends in jail. Most make the payments.

There are a number of benefits to restitution, besides the obvious one of paying back the victim. One is that for some offenders it makes real and vivid to them the loss that they caused to the victim, and it gives them an opportunity to make things right. They are able to deal with their guilt in a direct, constructive way. Studies have documented that recidivism rates of people ordered to pay restitution are at least as good as for similar people sent to prison, and in many cases are better.[6] This suggests that restitution may change offenders' attitudes.

A second benefit is that it can remove from our prisons many of the people currently there for nonviolent property offenses. We have seen that overcrowding is a critical problem. Almost half the people in our nation's prisons are there for nonviolent offenses. Many of them could have been ordered to pay restitution instead.

Experience has shown that this often does not happen, however, even when restitution programs exist.[7] Sometimes the only people ordered to pay restitution are the ones who would otherwise have gotten probation, not prison. It is important that states establishing restitution programs make it explicit that property offenders should not be imprisoned unless there are compelling reasons to do so (for example, if they refuse to comply with the restitution orders). States have done this through community corrections acts and sentencing guidelines.

An additional benefit is that the profit is removed from crime. Because few offenders actually receive (from sale) the full market value of the items stolen from the victim, offenders often have to pay back many times what they received. Profit prompted them to commit the crime in the first place; removing the profit is a powerful deterrent.

There are also, of course, limitations to restitution. For example, a few crimes involve money amounts that are so high that there is no practical way the offender will be able to pay back the victim. This raises two problems: what do we do with such offenders, and how do we respond to the needs of their victims? We will discuss victim compensation later. But there are several approaches to take with offenders who cannot pay. One is to order as much restitution as is practical, and then require that the offender perform services directly for the victims. An alternative is for the offenders to perform community service in order to repay the state for the amount of compensation it will pay the victim.

A second limitation is that this may result in different punishments for people convicted of identical offenses. For example, a burglary could result in the loss of $20 or $2,000. The amount of restitution will be based on the total loss to the victim.

This is fair. But what happens in cases where the losses are identical, but the offenders have different abilities to pay? Some may be able to make restitution out of money they have in the bank, whereas others will have to make installment payments for several years. Is this fair?

It is, if our principal objective is to restore the victim. There may, of course, be situations where the judge determines that additional punishment is needed because of the circumstances of the offense. In those cases the offender could be ordered to perform community service in addition to making the restitution payments.

Community Service

In November 1981, six inmates on furlough spent two weeks cleaning, insulating and weatherizing the homes of two widows living in urban Atlanta. The inmates were a part of Prison Fellowship's Community Service Project, a demonstration program showing how nonviolent offenders can be punished in ways that benefit the community.

Roxie Vaughn was one of the homeowners. She was 83, widowed and alone, and had been blind since birth. Her home had been burglarized four times in the last two years. She was reluctant to let the furloughed prisoners come.

But she needed help. Her drafty home was nearly impossible to heat in winter, and more and more of her social security checks were going to pay for fuel. So when she heard that the prisoners were Christians and that they wanted to insulate her home, she agreed to participate.

Over the two weeks her attic and cellar were insulated and her

doors and windows weatherstripped and caulked. And a healing relationship began to develop between her and the inmates. When
television crews came to cover the story at the end of the two weeks,
they found the house snug and warm and the six inmates singing
"Amazing Grace" and "Love Lifted Me" as Vaughn accompanied
them on her small electric organ.

Commentator Paul Harvey was so impressed with the project that
he wrote: "If nonviolent criminals, instead of being sentenced to
prison, can be sentenced to compulsory community service—or to
work in jobs until they make restitution to their victims and to the
state—then the punishment would fit the crime. And they would pay
taxes instead of taxpayers supporting them."

Prison Fellowship's program is simply a demonstration, a model, of
what community service sentencing offers as an alternative to judges.
Increasingly, judges are using this sentencing option.

Community service orders require the defendant to perform a specific number of hours of free work for a charitable or governmental
agency. Judges have ordered such sentences when there is no easily
identified victim, when restitution is impractical because of the offender's economic status, or when the judge wants to deal with the
harm caused to the community by the offense.[8]

The Probation Department for the District Court in Washington,
D.C., has operated a well-run community service program since 1977
with over one hundred fifty charitable and governmental agencies
participating.[9] The following description is based on it and other
successful programs around the nation.

As with restitution, community service orders must be specific. Offenders must know how many hours they are obligated to serve and
the amount of time they have to complete the requirement. In Washington the sentencing judge orders the total amount of work and the
time in which it is to be completed, and refers the defendant to the
Community Service Coordinator to make the appropriate placement.
In states where there is no formal community service program, a

specific work proposal is presented to the judge at sentencing, with letters of acceptance from the agencies which will be benefiting from the offender's work.

In most instances the community service order is one of the conditions of probation. In Washington, the typical offender is sentenced to serve between fifty and two hundred hours within one year. However, substantially higher sentences have been administered by the program. The probation officer explains the purpose of community service to offenders and then helps them identify their interests and abilities. As often as possible, offenders are assigned to those agencies that need their particular skills. Each offender then meets with an agency coordinator, and if both agree, the offender is assigned to the agency.

Because the offenders will be assigned to public agencies as part of their sentence, they must be carefully screened. In Washington most have been convicted of nonviolent offenses, although a few offenders have been admitted to the program following conviction for a violent crime. Experience has shown that drug users are not good candidates because of their high failure rate.

The agencies which receive community service placements in Washington are required to submit regular reports on the work of the offenders. As a result, the program costs little, since the agencies do the monitoring.

If offenders do not comply with the community service order, the probation staff meets with them to determine the reason. Sometimes the work agreement schedule needs to be modified, sometimes the offenders need to be assigned to new agencies, and sometimes they must be resentenced.

Experience has taught the staff of the community service program that it is not always solely the offender's fault when placement is unsuccessful. Sometimes offenders are asked to do work they cannot perform. Or there may be a personality conflict between the offender and the agency coordinator. To encourage offenders and agencies to report problems, the program permits offenders to change agencies during the course of their sentence, and the agency can request that an offender be transferred. Offenders are not sent to jail simply because the first placement was unsuccessful. However, offenders who do not complete their community service sentence may be sentenced to serve time in jail or prison.

The benefits of community service parallel some of the benefits of restitution. For certain offenders this kind of sentence can help change their values. Some find this to be one of the first times that they have done something, over a sustained period of time, which society considers constructive. A number of programs have reported that offenders continue to do free work even after the sentence has ended.

Although the sentence does not address the needs of a specific victim, it does give offenders a fairly direct way to "pay their debt to society." The inmates Prison Fellowship has used for its two-week community service projects have consistently said that they appreciate the opportunity to rehabilitate housing for others as a way of making up for their criminal activities. It has more meaning to them than sitting idle in prison.

Another benefit is that community service is a relatively low-cost sentence. A large number of people can be handled with minimal staff, since the agencies the offenders are working with are responsible for monitoring their performance.

Finally, it provides a tremendous resource to governmental and charitable organizations which need the abilities and expertise that the offenders bring. Of course, persons with professional skills can make those available where they would not be otherwise. For example, doctors can do free medical care in depressed parts of urban areas. Tradesmen can use their skills in repairing facilities that are run down. But less skilled laborers are also needed. They can provide the additional assistance that many agencies cannot afford to hire.

There are limitations to community service. It will not necessarily change the values of offenders. While it does give them an opportunity to help others who are often in more desperate straits than they, we have no guarantees that this will change their outlook.

And obviously community service does not directly benefit the victim of a crime. Where there is no specific victim (the so-called victimless crimes), this can be an appropriate substitute since it recognizes that the community is a secondary victim. But where there is a specific victim, community service clearly has limited value in addressing that victim's needs.

Victim-Offender Reconciliation

As we saw in part I, both victims and offenders are hurt by the lack of contact with each other after the crime. Victims need an opportunity to express anger and to ask questions. Offenders need the chance to acknowledge that their actions have hurt another person, to ask forgiveness, and to try to make amends. Our adversarial criminal justice system does not encourage this kind of interaction.

Several programs have been developed, however, which bring victims and offenders together at various stages in the criminal justice process. These have been remarkably successful.

All of these programs involve meetings of the victim and the offender in the presence of a trained mediator. The purpose of the meetings is to discuss the crime and the effects it has had on the victim and to attempt to structure a sentence proposal to offer to the judge. The programs are voluntary for both victims and offenders; most want to participate.[10]

Meetings take place at one of three points in the criminal justice process—before formal charges are filed, after the defendant is found guilty but before sentencing, or after a prison sentence but before the judge hears a motion to modify the sentence.

The *Cleveland Prosecutor Mediation Program* (CPMP) intervenes before formal charges are filed. The cases are usually misdemeanors, and they involve conflicts between people who know each other. Jerry

Kowalski and his adult son Walter were drinking together in Jerry's home. Walter had a history of drinking problems, and in the course of the evening he became drunk, lost his temper and threatened his father. Jerry called the police to file a complaint for assault.

Since Jerry lives in Cleveland, he and his son were referred to the CPMP. They were assigned one of the forty trained mediators who had them come to his office two weeks later. Each of them was given a chance to tell his story without interruption and the mediator helped them work out a settlement.

What satisfied both parties was for the son to apologize to his father and promise not to drink with him again. The mediator wrote down the agreement and had each of them sign it. After the father left, the mediator talked with the son about his drinking problem. The son agreed to seek counseling and join a treatment program.

The mediator then called both the father and son in two weeks to see that they were complying with the terms of the agreement. If they had not been, he would have referred the case to the prosecutor for charges to be filed.[11]

CPMP has proved to be popular and cost-effective. Since it was created the number of citizen-filed court complaints has dropped nearly fifty per cent. Instead of having to wait an average of 105 days and go to court three times to resolve the matter, the mediation hearing is held within 15 days of the complaint. Over ninety per cent of the people who used the program felt that the mediator had been fair; eighty-five per cent were satisfied with the results of the hearing; and seventy-seven per cent were still following the agreements one year later. The program handles 14,000 complaints each year.[12]

Victim Offender Reconciliation Programs (VORP) will intervene before trial, but more often they begin after the defendant has been found guilty but before sentencing. The results of the reconciliation meeting are considered by the judge in imposing sentence.

Pat Johnson had helped burglarize an apartment. The major property loss to the victim, David Knight, was a record collection. Some of the albums had been destroyed and others taken.

Johnson was caught and prosecuted. He turned the records over to the police. The case dragged on for months.

Both Knight and Johnson were becoming increasingly frustrated and angry. Knight insisted that he had gotten none of his albums back and that the collection was worth a great deal of money. Johnson and his parents felt that they were being had—that Knight was inflating the value of the collection and that the criminal justice process would drag on forever. At that point the case was referred to VORP.

The mediator first talked individually with all the parties. He located the albums, which had been misplaced in the police department. And then he brought Knight, Johnson and his parents together.

Both sides were finally able to express their feelings to each other. They were able to ask questions that had nagged at them and to have those questions answered. They began to understand each other. They agreed upon the cost of the losses, and Johnson made restitution on the spot. He also asked Knight to forgive him, which he did.[13]

VORPs were developed in Ontario, Canada, but are being successfully implemented in the United States. There are now programs in more than twenty states.[14]

They handle both misdemeanor and felony cases. In Elkhart, Indiana, for example, sixty per cent of the cases are felonies.[15] Most of these are burglary and theft cases, although an unusual VORP in upstate New York run by the Genesee County Sheriff's Department has handled violent crimes such as assault, armed robbery and negligent homicide.[16]

Victims and offenders are not required to meet, but they usually want to. Meetings take place in sixty-eight per cent of the cases.[17] And when they take advantage of the reconciliation process, victims and offenders are satisfied with the results. Eighty-six per cent of those surveyed were positive about the outcome.

The Post-Conviction Mediation Program,[18] run by the Oklahoma Department of Corrections, provides victim-offender reconciliation meetings after the defendant has been sentenced to prison.[19] It is one step in the development of something called the *Supervised Offender Accountability Plan* (SOAP). Under two different statutes, the Department of Corrections is required to prepare a plan for both nonviolent youthful offenders and all first-time offenders, which determines the amount of time offenders will serve in prison as well as the programs they should participate in. All the cases are felonies, and the most common are theft cases, although SOAP has handled violent crimes as well, such as manslaughter, rape and robbery.

One unique dimension of the program is its use of "victim representatives." When there is no specific victim, the program uses a surrogate. For example, in a case of drunk driving, a member of the state police may represent the interests of the police and the community in the mediation process.

Bill Richards had been convicted of burglary of a high school. He had taken shop tools and sports equipment. Although it was his first offense, he had received a two-year prison sentence.

The superintendent of the high school, Keith Adams, wanted to meet with Richards as the victim representative. He had been one of Richards's high-school teachers. So the Department of Corrections drove Richards two hundred fifty miles to the high school for the mediation session.

Adams explained how the loss of shop tools and sporting equipment had affected the students who attended the school. Richards had not thought about how his actions would hurt others. As they talked, he became increasingly remorseful and tearfully asked forgiveness. He and Adams agreed on a restitution payment schedule. He also agreed, at the superintendent's suggestion, to perform community service by doing groundskeeping work at the school. He felt that this conspicuous punishment would discourage others from doing what he had done.

When the SOAP plan was brought to the judge for consideration, Adams appeared in court to ask that the sentence be reduced to five months in prison, with the remainder to be served on intensive supervision to ensure that restitution payments were made. The judge was impressed with Adams's testimony and accepted the plan. Richards has successfully completed the community service and restitution agreement.

In its first year, one thousand victims were involved in the development of the SOAP sentencing plans. Seventy per cent of these wanted to meet with the offenders in mediation. In ninety-eight per cent of those cases, the victims were satisfied with the results. 32,000 hours of community service work have been arranged, restitution plans were established for over $300,000 and $13,000 has been raised for the State Crime Victim's Compensation Fund. The offenders who have been through the program are considered model probationers, and less than six per cent have failed to meet their agreements or have committed new crimes while under supervision.

Victim Compensation and Assistance

We saw in part I that victims experience loss in many ways. They have medical bills, lost income, property loss. But they also need help in working through their victimization and in going through the criminal justice process.

The offender should be principally responsible for meeting the out-of-pocket costs. Through restitution payments, the offender is held responsible and the victim repaid. But there are times when either the amount of the monetary loss or the kind of assistance the victim needs make it impossible for the offender to be able to respond.

Victim compensation. A 57-year-old Wisconsin woman was robbed and sexually assaulted at knifepoint by two intruders. She suffered physical injuries and experienced severe anxiety and loss of appetite. She wasn't able to work for twenty-one weeks.

What responsibility does the state have to provide for the financial losses suffered by crime victims? That was the questions that Margery Fry, a British magistrate, raised in 1957 in a highly influential article in the *London Observer*.[20] She argued that since the state forbids citizens to arm themselves in self-defense, it should take responsibility for their injuries when it fails to protect them from crime. Although most countries and states have rejected her rationale, a number have passed victim compensation laws.[21] The first such law was enacted in New Zealand in 1964, followed by Britain later that year.[22] In the U.S., California became the first state to pass such a bill (1965). By 1985, forty states had some form of victim compensation.[23]

Fortunately for the Wisconsin woman, her state was one of those with a compensation program. The Wisconsin Crime Victim Compensation Program authorized an emergency payment of $500 to cover her immediate expenses. A month later she received $753 to cover lost wages not reimbursed by disability pay, together with $50 for medical expenses that her insurance would not pay. The state also paid three subsequent medical bills, totaling $1,789.[24]

While programs vary from state to state, certain features appear to be uniform.[25] One is that only victims of violent crimes are reimbursed. Property losses are not covered. The intention of this exclusion is apparently to keep costs manageable. The programs also do not cover losses that have been reimbursed from other sources, such as insurance.

Most programs require the victim to report the crime to the police and to cooperate in the criminal justice process. Most require the victim to be a resident of the state, although increasingly states are signing reciprocal agreements with other states which have similar compensation schemes.

In addition, some of the programs compensate only victims who would suffer financial hardship, exclude victims who were a member of the offender's household, and require a minimum loss of at least $100. Most states also have limitations on the size of the awards—generally $10,000—although some like New York have no limit.

In late 1984 the federal government enacted legislation to provide funds for these state programs.[26] States which meet statutory requirements (including compensation for mental health counseling), are eligible to receive thirty-five per cent of whatever they had distributed to victims in the previous year. The money comes from fines collected from federal offenders, forfeited bail money, and all money received by federal offenders from books or movies based on their crimes.

Victim assistance. Victims need more than financial compensation in dealing with the aftermath of a crime. In response to this need, victim assistance programs have been established in every state. These range from rape crisis centers, to programs helping victims and witnesses deal with the complexities of the criminal justice process, to shelters for battered women. Some of these are privately funded, but many receive state funds or are a part of a state agency. The same federal legislation which funds compensation programs assists programs which meet the requirements (such as twenty-four-hour hotlines, use of volunteers, and so on). These programs can be tremendously helpful in restoring victims.

An elderly couple went to a bank in Washington, D.C., to cash their Social Security check. The money was essential to them—they needed it to buy groceries for the next month. As they walked out of the bank, they were held up by a gunman who took all their money. The police were called, but they were unable to locate any suspects.

The police referred the couple to the District's victim compensation program. But because they had not suffered any physical injury, the program was not able to help them. The staff suggested they go to a nearby victim assistance organization.

There they met with a victim advocate, a staff member who helps victims deal with the aftermath of the crimes they have suffered. The advocate called the Social Security office to see whether a replacement check could be issued. No reimbursement was possible, since the first check had been cashed.

So she began calling social agencies to see whether any of them could help the couple. One of those agencies was able to provide them with groceries. They would at least have food that month.

But the advocate did more than meet an immediate physical need. The couple had been traumatized by the experience. The crime happened quickly, they had been in great fear for their lives and they were worried about how they were going to survive the month before the next Social Security check. While she was locating groceries, the advocate let them talk about what they were feeling and assured them that their anger and fear were normal. When they left, they not only had received tangible assistance, but they felt better as well.[27]

No program can turn back the clock. The crime has occurred, and the victim (and offender) have to deal with that reality. But whether victims are able to reorganize (as we discussed in chapter 2) will depend to a great extent on the helpers and assistance available to them in the hours, days and months after the crime. Victim compensation and assistance programs can go a long way in this direction.

Real Life
Stephen Williams was eighteen years old. He and some friends from school had been breaking into houses all over town. They had stolen an estimated $150,000 worth of goods.

Their community was in an uproar. People did not know when they went home whether their houses would be safe. They worried about what might happen if the burglars caught someone at home. They invested in locks, guns and other self-defense measures.

The police were finally able to catch one of the burglars who implicated the others. They discovered that the teen-agers committed the crimes because they wanted to buy cars and maintain a high standard of living. They could make more money with less work by breaking into people's houses than they could by getting jobs.

There was considerable community pressure on the judge to give Steve and his codefendants substantial prison sentences. People were angry and wanted a forceful message sent to other students.

But the experienced judge noted that this was Steve's first arrest. "You now realize that you are not invulnerable," he told him. "And if there are other burglaries in the area, you know that yours will be one of the first doors the police knock on." He concluded that it was not likely that the youth would burglarize again.

"But you did break the law," he said, "and you must be punished. So my sentence has three parts."

First, Steve was required to perform community service every Saturday. He was required to work for the city, without pay, painting buildings, cleaning up the park and doing anything else that was needed. It was conspicuous punishment.

Second, he was ordered to pay restitution to his victims. That meant that he was to pay the market value of the items that he had taken and sold, which amounted to much more than he had gotten when he had fenced the goods. He was paying back multiple value when compared to what he had gained.

The judge gave him time to get a job and then took most of his paycheck for restitution payments. And because the judge wanted Steve to know what it was like to be burglarized, part of the restitution order was to sell all of his property and put the proceeds into the restitution fund.

Initially, the young man thought that meant only his car, which he had purchased with the proceeds of the crimes. It did mean the car, but it also meant *everything* else he owned, except for his clothes and his bed. It meant the trophy he had won at a track meet. It meant his baseball bat and glove. He had to sell everything he owned so he would understand that, to their owner, personal belongings have a greater worth than their market value.

The third part of the sentence was to sit down with the victims who wanted to talk to him about the crime. Steve said later that this was the toughest part of the sentence. He would rather have done anything else than meet with the people he had robbed. But he did it.

The victims were very angry. One couple had been collectors of antique oriental furniture for years and what Steve had taken was very valuable. But they had lost more than expensive furniture and art.

The antiques were also souvenirs of trips that the couple had taken together. For example, one of the stolen items was a Ming vase they had purchased ten years earlier at the end of a month-long vacation in Europe.

"Do you understand what you took from us?" they asked. "It was more than a beautiful, expensive vase. It was a reminder of our trip. Guests at our home would see the vase and admire it. We could tell them how we got the vase in a small shop in London at the end of our trip to Europe."

The young man was genuinely remorseful. He wanted to make it up to them somehow. The victims came up with a fascinating idea. They told him that as a down payment on his restitution he should go to an antique store and find something he thought they would like. If they agreed, then he would buy it for them.

So he went to several stores and finally found a beautiful oriental coffee table painted with black lacquer and a delicate flower design. He had found something that suited them and had showed them he was a sensitive young man, not simply a criminal.

The three of them have become friends. He mows their lawn. They talk to each other when they meet on the street. The young man has a sentence that will take him years to complete, but it is one that has meaning to him. The victims have been able to work through their fear and anger, and they are gradually having their losses restored. And although they lost one memento, they have gained another. Now when visitors come to their house and admire their coffee table, one of them says, "There is an interesting story about this coffee table . . ."

An offender held responsible for his action. Victims restored financially and emotionally. The community restored through the reconciliation of the offender and victims. This is a glimpse of *shalom*, a vision of what our communities can be.

Chapter 13

Restraining Criminals

George Bernard Shaw was indulging in hyperbole when he wrote these words. But his is an important warning:

Imprisonment as it exists today is a worse crime than any of those committed by its victims; for no single criminal can be as powerful for evil, or as unrestrained in its exercise, as an organized nation. Therefore, if any person is addressing himself to the perusal of this dreadful subject in the spirit of a philanthropist bent on reforming a necessary and beneficent public institution, I beg him to put it down and go about some other business. It is just such reformers who have in the past made the neglect, oppression, corruption, and physical torture of the old common gaol the pretext for transforming it into that diabolical den of torment, mischief, and damnation, the modern model prison.

If, on the contrary, the reader comes as a repentant sinner, let him read on.[1]

As we look at ways of improving punishment, we must remember Shaw's words. The Quakers and other reformers who originated the penitentiary system had idealistic motives. But look at the conditions Bradford Brown lived in during his imprisonment for a murder he did not commit.

We turn now to *restraint*, the kinds of controls that the state may exert to limit the freedoms (and perhaps end the lives) of criminal offenders.

Any court order puts restrictions on offenders. Probation places limitations on the people they may associate with and imposes a curfew, requirements of work, education and treatment programs, and so forth. There are also specific reporting requirements of probationers, which means that they must see the probation officer on a frequent basis. Probation officers may also visit them at work or school to be sure they are complying with the judge's order. Restitution orders restrict their use of material resources. Community service orders restrict their use of time and energy.

The question, then, is not *whether* there should be some restraint of criminals. It is how extensive the restraint should be. The general principle should be to exert the least amount that is necessary. But necessary to do what?

The Purpose of Restraint

The key thrust of the criminal justice system should be to hold the offender responsible for restoring the victim. Making the offender accept that responsibility is itself *retributive* and, as we have seen, is also often *rehabilitative*. If this is done swiftly and with reasonable certainty, it will *deter* others from committing crimes and will deter the offender as well.

But what restitution and community service do not do is fully *incapacitate* an offender known to pose an ongoing danger to the community. We saw earlier that there are problems with predicting accurately those who will commit new crimes, yet we know that there are such people. How do we deal with those we can identify?

There are several principles to keep in mind as we consider the options the state has before it. First, any punishment must fit the crime the person has committed, not the crimes we think he or she might commit in the future.

Second, as much as possible the restraint should not prevent the offender from restoring the victim, or providing for the needs of dependents.

Third, the degree of restraint should be reduced as the apparent likelihood of future criminal activity is reduced. An offender's values may change, and as they do, freedom should be increased.

Fourth, we must provide programs and services which will assist those offenders who wish to change.

With these principles in mind, let's look at the three main forms of restraint available to the state: community supervision, confinement and capital punishment.

Community Supervision

Historical precedents. We have already noted one of the predecessors of community supervision—the cities of refuge (Num 35:6-28).

Another historical precedent was known as "benefit of clergy."[2] In thirteenth-century England a number of crimes were punishable by death. To protect its clergy, the church insisted that it alone had jurisdiction over them, which allowed clerks, monks, priests and nuns to transfer their cases from the king's courts to the ecclesiastical courts which had much less severe penalties.

By the middle of the fourteenth century, the definition of "clergy" had been expanded to cover anyone who could read, and judges were willing to extend the benefit even to illiterate persons if they recited the required "neck verse" (so called because it saved them from being hanged):

Have mercy on me, O God,
  according to your unfailing love;
according to your great compassion
  blot out my transgressions. (Ps 51:1)

Eventually, because of abuses, its use was restricted to first-time offenders unless the defendant was actually a member of the clergy. It was abolished entirely in 1841.

That same year John Augustus, a cobbler in Boston, started asking judges to give him supervision over minor offenders. In an eighteen-year period he bailed out and supervised nearly two thousand men and women. This marked the beginning of our modern probation system.[3]

The first parole law was enacted twenty-five years later in New York. Parole was used to supervise the young men being released from their indeterminate sentences at Elmira Reformatory. Supervision lasted six months.[4]

Probation and parole. Today most people under some form of correctional supervision are on either probation or parole. During 1983 there were over 1.5 million people on probation in the United States, another 250,000 were on parole.[5] This far exceeds the 438,000 men and women in prison that year.[6]

The use of parole has diminished as the number of states using determinate sentences has increased. Concerned about the need for surveillance and support after the prison term has ended, some of those states (Illinois, for example) are requiring supervision for a period of time after release.

Probation and parole have been criticized as ineffective in preventing offenders from committing new crimes, particularly as more offenders have been placed on probation due to prison overcrowding. A report by the Rand Corporation in 1985 concluded that more than half of the most serious adult male probationers in their sample committed new crimes in the next forty months.[7]

This sample was clearly not representative of the probationers nationwide. First of all, the study focused on the thirty-five per cent of California's *probation* population whose characteristics were similar to those of most California *prisoners*.[8] Second, cases were drawn from two major urban areas where underfunding of probation offices had led to caseloads of three hundred probationers per probation officer. This is considerably higher than the model caseload of fifty.[9]

Intensive supervision. But the study underscored the need for close supervision of high-risk probationers. The recommendation of the Rand researchers was that states use intensive supervision for those serious offenders.

Intensive supervision is currently in use in eleven states. Although it varies from state to state, it is characterized by a low caseload for each probation officer, with probationers having a highly structured accountability program covering employment, treatment programs, community service and restitution, curfews and so forth. Probation officers meet with the probationers frequently, sometimes daily. Some meetings are scheduled and some are surprise visits to insure that the probationer is meeting the terms of the supervision order. The emphasis of the program is on surveillance, with rehabilitation having only secondary importance.[10] Although the cost of this kind of supervision is higher than normal probation, it is much less expensive than imprisonment. Moreover, it appears to be successful in reducing new crimes. A study of Georgia's intensive probation program recently showed that these more serious offenders committed new crimes at a much lower rate than released prisoners and at only a slightly higher rate than regular probationers.[11]

Confinement

Confinement can range from house arrest to halfway houses to total confinement in prison. Because of the exploding prison population, a number of states have been exploring ways of dealing with overcrowding. They have taken three basic approaches: build new prisons, decrease the number of people going into prisons, and reduce the sentences of certain less serious prisoners.

Prison construction. More than $2 billion is now being spent to construct new prisons.[12] This is an unprecedented construction program. But it is a fraction of what is needed if states intend to build their way out of the overcrowding problem. A 1981 study determined that more than *$10 billion* was necessary to create sufficient space for the prisoners that year.[13] Since then the prison population has increased by nearly a hundred thousand.

Diversion. The second approach states have taken is to develop new penalties in addition to prison and standard probation. They have done this in light of evidence that a significant portion of the prison population may not need to be incarcerated to ensure public safety. The principle that there should be no more restraint than is necessary has led these states to conclude that new penalties could provide for the restoration of the victim without jeopardizing the safety of the community.

A 1979 survey of state inmates revealed that approximately two out of every ten inmates sent to prison had no prior adult conviction.[14] Only fifty-five per cent of those admitted to prison were sent for a violent offense or had previously served time for a violent offense.[15] States confronted with severe overcrowding have begun paying close attention to what kinds of offenders are going to their prisons. The results have been surprising.

Indiana discovered, for example, that twenty per cent of its inmates were first offenders convicted of nonviolent crimes. The cost of keeping them in prison was $20 million per year, not counting welfare costs for their dependents.[16] As a result, the state began developing other punishments to keep those offenders out of prison, but under *close supervision.* The result was the Community Corrections Act, which provides money to local counties to establish restitution, community service and work-release programs for nonviolent, first-time offenders. The program has worked so well that the legislature has doubled its funding with each state budget to a current total of $6 million. In part because of its success, the prison population in Indiana, which grew twenty per cent in 1981, had no significant growth in 1984.[17] Twelve other states have developed similar community corrections programs.

States have also developed *sentencing guidelines,* designed to provide judges with standard sentences for similar offenders convicted of the same offense. Guidelines help avoid "sentencing disparity," in which prisoners convicted of the same crime and with similar backgrounds are sentenced to different terms simply because they appeared before different judges.

But sentencing guidelines have also been used to ensure that scarce prison space is used for more serious offenders and that less serious offenders are put in community corrections. Minnesota has been the leader with this use of guidelines and has been able to keep its prison population within capacity while ensuring that serious offenders are locked up.[18]

Early release. The third approach is to reduce the sentences of less serious offenders when prisons are overcrowded. One method of doing this has been through *emergency release acts.* Michigan, for example, established a procedure for making prisoners eligible for parole ninety days early whenever the prisons are full. The Parole Commission is then able to grant early release to offenders who do not pose a risk to the community. At least three other states have similar laws.

Some states have adopted a different approach. They have used the research on *risk assessment* (discussed in chapter 7) to identify the prisoners least likely to get in trouble again and have set up parole guidelines designed to release them early without endangering the public. Georgia's parole board, for example, claims a 99.2 per cent success rate in identifying inmates who are not likely to commit new crimes and who therefore can be released when overcrowding begins to occur because of new prisoners.[19]

It has been estimated that American prisons are at least ten per cent over their normal capacity.[20] Far more than ten per cent of the offenders there pose minimal danger to society. Through community corrections, sentencing guidelines, and sentence reduction methods for low-risk prisoners, states are finding it possible to control prison overcrowding without expensive prison construction, while punishing offenders by making them pay back their victims and provide services to their communities.

Other needed reforms. Solving the overcrowding crisis would be a tremendous step toward improving the conditions in American prisons. But there are other important changes to make as well. These have been set out at length elsewhere,[21] so I will only mention some of the more obvious ones: adequate classification of inmates to separate predators from their prey, improved training and compensation for prison staff, vocational and training programs to prepare the prisoner for life outside, religious programs and other services to provide alternative value systems for offenders, re-entry programs of furloughs and halfway houses, grievance procedures to respond to systemic problems, and conjugal visits and other programs designed to preserve family relationships.

While we cannot expect miracles, such programs go a long way toward making prison a less debilitating experience. That would be good for all of us.

Capital Punishment

One of the most pressing criminal justice issues today is capital punishment. More than fifteen hundred men and women were on death row at the end of 1985. The court-imposed moratorium on executions which had been in effect since the 1960s has ended. If the current trend continues, the country will soon witness daily executions.

Christians are divided on the issue. For some, the provisions of the Mosaic Law calling for the death penalty settle the issue. Others question the ethics of the death penalty on the basis of Jesus' words and actions and the lack of explicit teaching in the New Testament. The more pragmatic believers explore the practical issues of whether it deters crime and whether there is a serious risk of executing innocent people.

Part of the problem is that we do not have a common approach to discussing the issue. I'd like to suggest that we consider this topic by asking three questions:

1. Does Scripture prohibit, mandate or permit capital punishment? If Scripture prohibits it, the next two questions are irrelevant. But if it does not, then a second question must be raised.

2. According to Scripture, under what conditions may a state exercise capital punishment? After exploring these conditions, those who hold that Scripture merely permits (rather than mandates) capital punishment must proceed to the third question.

3. What principles should guide the state in determining whether to exercise the death penalty?[22]

Let's look at each of these questions.

1. Is capital punishment mandated, prohibited or permitted? The principle argument of those who hold that it is *mandated* is that life is sacred and those who take another life must lose their own. It is a form of restitution. They find scriptural support in three major areas.

First, Genesis 9:6 says: "Whoever sheds the blood of man, by man shall his blood be shed; for in the image of God has God made man." This excerpt from the covenant God made with Noah after the flood not only demonstrates the great value of human life, but it also gives the reason for that value—man is made in God's image.

Second, the Law contained a number of provisions calling for capital punishment. (We noted this in chapter 10.)

Third, while the New Testament does not explicitly mandate capital punishment, several passages imply its use. For example, Paul calls his readers to submit to the authority of civil government, reminding them, "If you do wrong, be afraid, for [the governing authority] does not bear the sword for nothing" (Rom 13:4). In its ultimate use, the sword can be used to execute wrongdoers.

Those who believe that Scripture *prohibits* capital punishment argue that developments in the New Testament era supercede Old Testament Law.

First, they note that Israel was a unique nation called by God to a unique role. (Many of the provisions in the Law calling for executions were for violating religious requirements designed to keep the nation holy.) When Israel ceased to be a nation, they argue, its Law was nullified.

Second, Christ's death on the cross ended the requirement for blood recompense. The death of Christ forever established man's value, and execution of murderers is no longer needed to serve that purpose.

Third, Christ's teaching emphasizes forgiveness and a willingness to suffer evil rather than resist it by force. To those demanding the death of the woman taken in adultery (Jn 8:1-11), Jesus responded by challenging their own sinfulness and lack of charity.

Others reconcile the arguments of the mandators and the prohibitionists by holding that Scripture *permits* the use of capital punishment.

First, both Testaments must be considered. The Old Testament provision calling for capital punishment was given first to Noah (Gen 9:6), long before the Mosaic Law was given. New Testament references to capital punishment are ambiguous. The passages dealing with it clearly assume its existence, but do not address the question of whether it is required. Even Romans 13, cited earlier, refers only to the *authority* of the state to execute, not its *obligation* to do so.

Second, there are a number of examples in both Testaments of capital criminals who were *not* executed, clearly with God's approval. After Cain killed Abel, God not only spared his life, but protected him from others who might kill him. David committed two capital crimes, adultery and murder, but God did not demand his life. Christ did not insist on the execution of the woman taken in adultery. Paul urged Philemon to accept his runaway slave Onesimus back into his household, even though Roman law provided for execution.

I am a lawyer. While I am impressed with the arguments of those who hold the death penalty to be mandated or prohibited, there are two principles of understanding law which should help us here. The first is that we must avoid interpreting documents in a way that creates internal contradictions. Yet that is in essence what happens when prohibitionists interpret the New Testament as superceding the Old and prohibiting something which was allowed in the Old Testament.

Second, case law is also an important source of our understanding of the law. When we take the cases of Cain, David, the adulterous woman and Onesimus together with Genesis 9:6 and the sixth commandment, the most reasonable conclusion is that Scripture permits, but does not mandate, the death penalty.

2. What scriptural conditions govern the state's use of this power? As we have seen in chapter 10, the Law provided not only the substantive Law and penalties for disobeying it, but also the procedures for carrying out the Law. We have discussed some of these earlier, but let us review the principles which governed capital cases.

First, punishment was to be proportionate to the crime. It was not to exceed the crime. Death, therefore, should be considered only in the most serious offenses.

Second, there must be certainty of guilt. The Law required the testimony of two eyewitnesses before the accused could be put to death (Num 35:30; Deut 17:6). This was actually a higher standard of proof than for other criminal cases.[23]

Third, there must have been an intent to kill. We have seen how the cities of refuge were used to protect those who committed manslaughter.

Fourth, there must be due process. There was to be a fair trial, the trial was to be supervised by qualified officials, and certainty of guilt had to be reached by a specific technical procedure (Num 35; Deut 17:8-9).

Fifth, only the person responsible for the crime could be executed (Deut 24:16).

Sixth, the trial was to be fair. There was to be equal justice regardless of the economic or social status of the accused (Ex 23:6-7; Num 35:29-31).

And finally, Scripture reveals God's reluctance to execute. He exercised mercy in many cases, saying, "As surely as I live . . . I take no pleasure in the death of the wicked, but rather that they turn from their ways and live" (Ezek 33:11; see also Hos 11:8-9).

If we look at laws in the United States concerning the death penalty and compare them to these principles, we see, first, that some biblical principles are recognized in U.S. practice. Legal challenges of specific death penalty statutes have reflected many of these ideas. Following the principle of *proportionality*, for example, the Supreme Court has prohibited execution in cases of rape. The principle of *fairness* was also recognized, since the overwhelming majority of those who had been executed for rape were minorities.[24] Another case held that a codefendant driving the getaway car during a robbery could not be executed for murder committed by one of the other offenders if he did not kill the victims himself, did not intend to kill them, and did not attempt to kill them. This reflects the principles of *intent* and *individual responsibility*.[25] One of the key reasons that all capital punishment statutes were declared unconstitutional in 1972 was that they did not have sufficient standards to prevent racial inequities. They lacked *fairness*.[26] And there were overtones of *reluctance* in a 1976 case which ruled that mandatory death penalty laws were unconstitutional because they did not allow courts to consider mitigating factors.[27]

But, second, we also see that current death penalty statutes do not incorporate all biblical principles, particularly *certainty of guilt, fairness* and *reluctance*. In a number of cases, defendants who had been sentenced to death were later pardoned when someone else confessed or when they received new trials and were acquitted.[28] Although Bradford Brown was not sentenced to death (the District of Columbia does not have a death penalty statute), his case reminds us that our legal system does sometimes convict the wrong man.

And while there have been important reforms in sentencing procedures, evidence remains that the death penalty still is applied in a racially discriminatory way. A recent study found that the death sentence is most often imposed when a black person kills a white person. Whites who kill whites are sentenced to death one-third less often, and only a small fraction of people (black or white) who kill blacks are given the death sentence.[29]

Finally, there seems to be a growing desire to execute. Courts are imposing the death penalty more often than ever before. Between 1930 and 1972, approximately 3,860 persons were executed (a rate of 92 per year). Since 1976, 1,500 have been sentenced to death (a rate of over 180 per year). While most of these men and women have not yet been executed (due to appeals), the courts and legislatures have concluded that they should be put to death. It is simply a matter of time before their sentences are carried out.[30]

These shortcomings raise substantial questions that Christians must consider seriously before supporting any of the existing death penalty laws.

If we assume, nevertheless, that those laws can be improved so as to incorporate biblical standards, we are presented with the third question.

3. What principles should guide the state in determining whether to use the death penalty? Those of us who believe the death penalty is permitted must consider this third question. Here the key issue is whether there is a unique benefit to using the death penalty, or whether other, less severe, penalties will accomplish the same purposes.

Christians have sought this kind of balance on similar issues, such as that of just war. Most Christians regard war as evil in principle, but justifiable under certain circumstances. If war is the only way to protect innocent people from hostile aggressors, many Christians believe that it is acceptable.

Capital punishment may be justified if it is practiced in harmony with the biblical standards we have just reviewed, and if it achieves good purposes which cannot be reached in any other way. The three purposes most often given are general deterrence, specific deterrence and punishment.

General deterrence is the theory that when one person is punished for his crime, others will not commit that crime for fear of getting the same punishment. As we have seen earlier, this has been a very difficult theory to prove. In fact, the overwhelming majority of studies has shown that capital punishment does not deter murder.[31]

The Bible does not give deterrence as a reason for executing murderers. The three cases in which it does give deterrence as a reason for the death penalty are willful contempt of court (Deut 17:12-13), willfully giving false testimony in a capital case (Deut 19:16-21) and persistent rebellion of children against their parents (Deut 21:18-21). Each of these requires premeditation, a prerequisite of deterrence.

If it can be shown that the death penalty does deter murder, this will be a powerful argument for capital punishment. To date, however, this has not been established.

Specific deterrence is beyond dispute: execution prevents the offender from committing other crimes. This is obvious, but the question remains whether such an extreme sanction is needed to achieve this purpose. Imprisoning murderers for life under appropriate security and surveillance also prevents them from killing.

We have talked throughout this book about the importance and appropriateness of *punishment*. Those who emphasize its importance say that it is irrelevant whether the death penalty deters. The law must be established by penalizing its violators.

But some who believe in punishment reject capital punishment as the most appropriate form because of the possibility of executing innocent persons. They suggest that imprisonment punishes as well or better than execution.

Conclusion

So what is the Christian perspective on capital punishment? Is it mandated, prohibited or permitted? Do current statutes meet biblical standards? Does it offer practical benefits?

Although my intention has been to propose an *approach* to discussing those questions, I suspect that my own biases have come through.[32] I believe that the state is permitted to execute murderers when specific conditions have been met. They have not been met as of this writing. And, even if those conditions can be met, I would oppose exercising this authority unless convincing evidence of deterrence can be found. There may be some instances in which we currently come close to achieving both biblical standards and evidence of deterrence (for example, when a prisoner already serving a life sentence kills a guard without provocation and in front of two or more witnesses). But these are few and far between.

Chapter 14

Where Do We Go from Here?

Ross Osborn *manages* an insurance agency in Evansville, Indiana. For years he had been concerned about the problems in the criminal justice system. His previous experience as an FBI agent had made him aware that changes were desperately needed. His Christian commitment convinced him that biblical principles addressed those problems.

"I would read in the paper about a woman stealing bread to feed her children. She's caught three times and gets a long sentence as an 'habitual offender.' Then I'd wonder—what good will it do to put her in prison? So many come out worse than when they went in."[1]

By 1981 this kind of indiscriminate sentencing had helped create an unprecedented overcrowding crisis in Indiana. Its prison population had doubled in the previous six years. The population increased by twenty per cent in 1981 alone. The governor was considering a $200 million prison construction program.

What could one man do? Osborn looked for ways to get involved in promoting the changes he knew were necessary for the state. He contacted Justice Fellowship (JF), an advocacy organization affiliated with Prison Fellowship Ministries. As it turned out, Justice Fellowship had recently been approached by Senate Judiciary Committee chairman Leslie Duvall and Senator Bill Costas for materials on diverting nonviolent offenders from prison. As JF researched the problems that Indiana was facing, they found genuine interest among public officials to take steps toward solving the crisis. In 1980 the legislature had created a pilot community corrections program in three counties with funding of $250,000. This looked promising but was woefully inadequate to meet the urgent prison crowding crisis.

So in 1982 JF convened a task force of Indiana Christians, chaired by Dr. Milo Rediger, president emeritus of Taylor University, to advocate community service and restitution programs for nonviolent offenders who would otherwise go to prison.

Ross Osborn was one of the fifteen people who joined Dr. Rediger in the effort. The task force set two objectives, and they agreed to pursue these for a three-year period. First, they would create public support for substantial increases in the budget for these programs. Second, they would attempt to persuade local officials, who were somewhat skeptical, to use these programs.

They pursued these goals with determination. They wrote articles and made speeches. They spent hours meeting with legislators, judges and corrections officials. They visited a number of the state's prisons and the community corrections programs. They contacted county officials to let them know what they were discovering.

In 1983 the legislature passed a $2.8 million budget for community corrections—more than ten times the budget for 1981. So many counties became interested in the program that additional funding was needed. In 1985, the legislature approved a new budget of $6 million.

The Secretary of State of Indiana, Edwin Simcox, commented on the impact of the task force.

I have seen the influence of the task force on the general assembly—actually on the development of public policy. Now there are a lot of groups and organizations and associations who take credit for passage or defeat of a piece of legislation. I regulate the lobbyists in this state and the more than three million dollars that are spent on lobbying activities. There are not many of them that really do [influence] public policy.

But in this instance, with this task force and in the matter of criminal justice reform, I can say that the legislature listened. They influenced public policy.[2]

For Ross Osborn there is a lesson in this experience. "I've learned that a state is not too big a place to get changes made." Not when people work together.

Action You Can Take

Most of us, faced with the problems in the criminal justice system, ask the same question Osborn did: What can *I* do? The issue is complex, the system is overwhelming, and the possibility of making a difference seems remote. But change is possible. There are a number of specific steps each of us can take to offer constructive assistance. (Addresses for organizations mentioned here can be round in the resource section in Appendix A.)

First, become informed. Are the prisons in your state overcrowded? Are there effective victim assistance and compensation programs in operation? Are most nonviolent offenders punished through community service programs? (One way to check this is to see what percentage of the prison population consists of nonviolent offenders.)

1. Contact your state representatives and ask them for information. You can get the names and addresses of your representatives by checking at your local library or local newspaper or by calling the state capital.

2. Write or call an advocacy organization listed in the resources section for their analysis of the situation in your state. For example, Justice Fellowship has a statistical analysis of each state which provides members with current information on a number of key issues. The National Organization for Victim Assistance distributes excellent resource materials to support its annual victims' rights campaigns.

3. Read the newspaper and start a file of the useful articles. These will not only give you an accurate idea of what is happening in your state, but they will also let you know who the key officials are.

4. Visit a nearby prison or jail. You pay for these institutions with tax money, and you should be interested in seeing what is happening with that money. Call your local sheriff or the state department of corrections to see how you can tour a facility.

5. If there is a community service, restitution or victim assistance program in your city, call the administrator. Ask for written materials describing what they do. Find out whether you can visit and whether they have speakers available to make presentations at churches or other organizations.

6. Get involved as a volunteer. Firsthand knowledge is the best kind, and you will also be performing an important service. Your neighborhood may have a citizen watch program. If so, get involved. If not, talk to your neighbors about organizing one. The National Crime Prevention Council can send you information on how to do this.

Prison ministries rely heavily on volunteers. The Institute for Prison Ministries of the Billy Graham Center in Wheaton, Illinois, publishes a directory of prison ministries, and you may want to contact one in your area.

Victim assistance groups are required to use volunteers to qualify for federal support. The National Organization for Victim Assistance publishes a directory of victim assistance groups throughout the country. Volunteer with one in your city.

7. Sit in a courtroom for an afternoon to watch how cases are

handled and how victims and criminals are treated.

8. Talk to the police about crime prevention programs in your area. They will be able to tell you about neighborhood crime watch programs and how you can get involved with them.

9. Read a book on the victimization experience. (See the resource section for ideas.)

10. Read a book on prisons. (See the resource section.)

Second, find other people to work with. Some people are happy working on long-term projects by themselves. Most of us are not. We need the encouragement, the ideas and the friendship that a team brings.

11. Join an advocacy organization. A number of national groups are listed in the resources section. But there are also many effective local groups. Ask your state representatives to suggest ones they recommend.

12. Contact your denomination to see whether it has a staff person or committee working on criminal justice issues. Many of the mainline denominations have representatives on the National Inter-religious Task Force on Criminal Justice. It can refer you to the staff person in your denomination.

13. Talk with your Bible study or Sunday-school class about taking this on as a group project. One person can watch the local newspapers for interesting articles about the criminal justice system. Then the whole group can write letters to your legislators or the newspapers when important issues come up.

Third, let other people know how you feel. Everyone has a circle of people that he or she influences. Who are the people who pay attention to your ideas? They probably have not done serious thinking about the problems in criminal justice, and they will be curious about what you have discovered. Let them know what you have found and ask them to help.

14. Teach a course on criminal justice in your church. Several resources are available, including a multiweek course called *Crime and Community in Biblical Perspective* (see the resource section for details).

15. Write a letter to a public official. Most people never write or call their elected officials. As a result, your representatives will pay attention to you when you do contact them.

16. Write your local newspaper and radio and television stations. Many of them will print or broadcast your views, which will help influence other concerned people in your community.

17. Invite an expert to speak at your church or civic organization. You can contact your local victim assistance program, prison ministry, prosecutor, public defender or community corrections program for suggestions.

18. Talk with your pastor about programs that assist victims and offenders. Pastors are often contacted for help by people caught up in the criminal justice process, and they should be aware of the resources that are available.

19. Offer to speak at your church or civic organization.

Finally, pray. Include victims, offenders, public officials and the people working in the criminal justice system in your daily prayers. Scripture encourages us to pray for our leaders, and to pray for the peace and prosperity of the place in which we live. As you study Scripture to learn more about the justice, holiness, love and mercy of God, ask him to give you the energy and dedication to be his servant in this important area.

Organizations That Can Help

There are tremendous resources available to public officials and citizens in the area of criminal justice. The resource section lists some of the national organizations. In addition there are excellent groups with local or regional scopes. The directories mentioned in point 6 will refer you to ones in your area.

What follows is a brief description of several of the national programs. My aim here is simply to illustrate the breadth of services available to you as you start working.

Prison Fellowship Ministries (PFM) was established in 1976 by Charles

Colson. Its purpose is to assist churches in ministry with prisoners, ex-prisoners and their families. This ministry to prisoners is conducted through volunteers, trained and assisted by PFM staff. These volunteers participate in seminars inside and out of prisons, where inmates participate in Bible study and religious training. PFM also assists families of prisoners and helps ex-prisoners in the transition to life outside.

Two unique programs symbolize key facets of Prison Fellowship Ministry's activities. The first is the Community Service Seminar, in which inmates are furloughed from prison for Bible study and to help in a community project such as rehabilitating a home. The other is Project Angel Tree which takes place each Christmas. Volunteers contact the families of prisoners to find out what the young children in the family would like for Christmas. They then fasten these requests to a Christmas tree placed in a shopping mall or church, and passersby purchase the gifts. The volunteers then distribute the presents on Christmas Eve.

Justice Fellowship, which is affiliated with PFM, has already been mentioned. It lobbies for restitution and community service punishments for appropriate offenders, victim assistance and compensation programs, reconciliation opportunities for victims and offenders, and fair and effective use of prison for those offenders who must be incarcerated. JF works at both the state and federal levels, meeting with legislators and governors and conducting state-wide public education campaigns similar to the one Ross Osborn worked on in Indiana.

Justice Fellowship is a membership organization. Members receive the newsletter, *The Justice Report*, updates on activities in their states, and periodic legislative alerts.

The *Office on Criminal Justice of the Mennonite Central Committee* (OCJ/MCC) is an education and resource program working through Mennonite as well as other churches. It distributes booklets, posters, slide sets, and its newsletter, *Network*. It holds periodic consultations—workshops with a speaker and a small number of participants to explore facets of the criminal justice system. For example, Herman Bianchi, a Dutch scholar who has done groundbreaking research in Old Testament "criminal" justice processes, was the guest at a recent consultation.

The OCJ/MCC has been closely identified with the development of Victim-Offender Reconciliation Programs. The Canadian branch developed the concept of VORPs and ran the first programs. The United States office has not run any VORPs itself, but it has been instrumental in promoting and assisting such programs. The OCJ/MCC focuses most of its energies on programs for individuals in the hope that public policy will change in response to the examples these programs offer.

The *National Organization for Victim Assistance* (NOVA) is an advocacy organization working with victim and witness assistance practitioners, criminal justice professionals, researchers, former victims and others who are interested in promoting the rights of victims in the criminal justice system.

It lobbies for victim-oriented legislation in state legislatures as well as in Congress. It played a key role in the development of the federal Victim-Witness Protection Act as well as the legislation which established federal grants to local assistance and compensation programs. NOVA supports this legislative activity with extensive public education and sponsors an annual campaign for victims rights which each year focuses on a particular area of need.

NOVA also serves victims and witnesses directly, and it helps establish local assistance programs and provide technical services for them. It publishes an annual directory of those programs.

NOVA is a membership organization. Members receive the monthly newsletter and are invited to participate in national conferences.

The *Presbyterian Criminal Justice Program* (PCJP) is unique among mainline denominational programs in that it has a full-time staff member assigned to it. The office serves Presbyterians in two ways:

by providing resource materials and consultations to churches, and by representing denominational policies in both ecumenical and secular arenas. The denomination has taken stands on capital punishment, on ministry to victims of crime, and on the need to reduce incarceration.

PCJP publishes a newsletter, *Justice Jottings*, three times a year. It also has developed resource materials on several of the denomination's major areas of concern in the criminal justice system: juvenile justice, capital punishment, victims, and fear of crime. These resources are available for individual use or for group discussion.

One of its most interesting activities is the annual commemoration of Criminal Justice Sunday, which is held on the second Sunday in February. The purpose of the day is to draw attention to the criminal justice system and to give the churches the opportunity for reflection and prayer. The theme of the Sunday changes annually and has addressed, for example, victimization and fear of crime.

Among *Catholic churches,* prison ministry is often overseen by the local diocese where the facility is located. For example, the priests at Colby House in Chicago work as chaplains in four facilities in the Chicago archdiocese, including federal, state and local prisons. They minister directly with prisoners, offering religious services, counseling, religious education classes, Bible studies and group programs. Those interested in hearing more about Catholic ministry in local prisons can contact the administrative office of their diocese.

Conclusion

In life we are often presented with false choices and dilemmas. The area of criminal justice is no exception. Should we punish criminals or forgive them? Should we love them or their victims? Should we solve prison overcrowding or work to prevent crime? These are not the true issues.

It is in the prayer of the Israelite prophet Jeremiah that I see the real choices:

Correct me, LORD, but only with justice—
 not in your anger,
 lest you reduce me to nothing. (Jer 10:24)
We must decide whether criminal punishment is governed by justice or anger.

The American people are angry about crime. And for good reason. Our communities are threatened. Yet a criminal justice policy built on anger not only destroys offenders but ultimately destroys the community. It destroys us financially, and it destroys us morally.

Gerald Austin McHugh, in *Christian Faith and Criminal Justice*, speaks of Jesus' command that we love our enemies.[3] He suggests that criminals are our enemies. Admitting that helps us in several ways. First, it is realistic. Jesus did not say, "Do not have enemies." He assumed that we would have them. What he told us to do was love them.

I find it helpful to talk about the persons who broke into my home as my enemies. That really is how I feel about them. They took more from me than personal property. They also took my sense of security and my trust that the world is basically a friendly place.

Second, McHugh points out that *enemy* is a relational term. I know where I stand with my enemies: I know whether I have been reconciled, whether I am loving them or hating them. The terminology recognizes the truth that there is a relationship, even though it is a destructive one and even though (for me) it was an involuntary one.

When Jeremiah asked God to correct him, he had sinned. He had made himself an enemy to God. He knew that judgment was coming and was deserved. He cried not for mercy, but for justice. He did not expect in his pleas to be forgiven, but he knew that justice would restrain and direct the judgment and restore him to a right relationship with God.

Many of the prisoners I talk to are, in effect, saying the same thing. They have broken the law and must pay the price. But what a price to pay! They are locked up in crowded, violent prisons. When they are released they find that often they cannot vote, many jobs are closed to them, and even some churches do not want them as members.

Chief Justice Warren Burger has said that we have a correctional system that does not correct. Many people—inmates, victims and average citizens—also believe that we have a criminal justice system that is not just. That has led to frustration.

Shall we correct with anger or with justice? We can pass tough laws, raise taxes for new prisons, and hope we are not victimized further. Or we can work together for a new approach in criminal justice, one which holds offenders responsible for restoring their victims.

That is the real choice.

Appendix A: Resources

The following list of organizations and books is certainly not exhaustive, but it should give you a good overview of the resources that are available. Both lists have been organized into areas of primary emphasis.

Organizations
The organizations listed do not all agree with each other. For example, the National Prison Project of the ACLU appears in the same section as the American Correctional Association. But the first sues prison systems over their conditions of confinement and the second is the professional association of those who run the prisons. Do not assume that groups have been listed together because they agree. They are linked because of their common concerns.

It might be helpful to contact a number of these organizations and ask for materials which explain their work. This will help you determine which ones you would like to become more involved in.

Organizations
1. Prison Ministries
Bill Glass Ministries, P.O. Box 356, Dallas, TX 75221. Phone: 214/291-7895.
Coalition of Prison Evangelists, 901 Louisiana Ave., Shreveport, LA 71101. Phone: 318/226-9393.
Good News Mission, International Headquarters, 1036 South Highland Street, Arlington, VA 22204. Phone: 703/979-2200.
Institute for Ministry to Prisoners, Billy Graham Center, Wheaton College, Wheaton, IL 60187. Phone: 312/260-5157. The institute does not conduct prison ministry itself, but is a training and resource center for Christians interested in ministering in prisons.
International Prison Ministries, P.O. Box 63, Dallas, TX 75221. Phone: 800/527-1212.
Prison Fellowship International, P.O. Box 17434, Washington, DC 20041. Phone: 703/481-0000. This organization does not conduct prison ministry, but charters and assists national Prison Fellowships around the world.

Prison Fellowship Ministries—USA, P.O. Box 17500, Washington, DC 20041. Phone: 703/478-0100.

Yokefellows International Prison Ministry, 1200 Almond Street, Williamsport, PA 17701. Phone: 717/326-6868.

2. Victim Assistance and Advocacy Organizations

Mothers Against Drunk Driving, 669 Airport Freeway, Suite 310, Hurst, TX 76053. Phone: 817/268-MADD.

National Organization for Victim Assistance, 1757 Park Road N.W., Washington, DC 20010. Phone: 202/393-6682.

Parents of Murdered Children, 1739 Bella Vista, Cincinnati, OH 45237. Phone: 513/721-5683.

3. Criminal Justice Reform Advocacy Organizations

Judicial Reform Project, Committee for the Survival of a Free Congress, 721 Second Street NE, Washington, DC 20002. Phone: 202/546-3004.

Justice Fellowship, P.O. Box 17181, Washington, DC 20041. Phone: 703/759-9400.

NAACP Legal Defense Fund, 99 Hudson Street, New York, NY 10013. Phone: 212/219-1900.

National Center on Institutions and Alternatives, 814 North Saint Asaph Street, Alexandria, VA 22314. Phone: 703/684-0373.

National Coalition Against the Death Penalty, 1324 Walnut Street, Philadelphia, PA 19107. Phone: 215/592-1513.

National Council on Crime and Delinquency, 77 Maiden Lane, Fourth Floor, San Francisco, CA 94108. Phone: 415/956-5651.

National Moratorium on Prison Construction, 309 Pennsylvania Avenue SE, Washington, DC 20003. Phone: 202/547-3633.

PACT Institute of Justice, 106 North Franklin, Valparaiso, IN 46383. Phone: 219/464-1400.

Southern Coalition on Jails and Prisons, P.O. Box 120044, Nashville, TN 37212. Phone: 615/242-5131.

4. Prison Advocacy and Professional Organizations

American Correctional Association, 4321 Hartwick Road, Suite L-208, College Park, MD 20740. Phone: 301/699-7600.

Correctional Education Association, 1400 20th Street NW, Washington, DC 20036. Phone: 202/293-3120.

National Prison Project, American Civil Liberties Union, 1616 "P" Street NW, Suite 340, Washington, DC 20036. Phone: 202/331-0500.

5. Denominational/Religious Organizations

Association for Public Justice, 806 15th Street NW, Room 218, Washington, DC 20005. Phone: 202/737-2110.

Friends Committee on National Legislation, 245 2nd Street NE, Washington, DC 20002. Phone: 202/547-6000.

National Inter-religious Task Force on Criminal Justice, 475 Riverside Drive, JSAC Office, New York, NY 10015. Phone: 212/870-3105.

Office of Criminal Justice, Mennonite Central Committee, 220 West High Street, Elkhart, IN 46516. Phone: 219/293-3090.

Presbyterian Criminal Justice Program, 475 Riverside Drive, Room 1244, New York, NY

10115. Phone: 212/870-3143.

6. Crime Prevention Organizations

Criminal Justice Services, American Association of Retired Persons, 1909 "K" Street NW, Washington, DC 20049. Phone: 202/728-4363.

National Association of Town Watch, P.O. Box 769, Havertown, PA 19083. Phone: 215/ 649-6662.

National Crime Prevention Council, 733 15th Street NW, Suite 540, Washington, DC 20005. Phone: 202/393-7141.

7. Criminal Justice Information Organizations

CONtact Center, Inc., P.O. Box 81826, Lincoln, NE 68501. Phone: 402/464-0602.

National Criminal Justice Reference Service, National Institute of Justice/NCJRS, P.O. Box 6000, Rockville, MD 20850. Phone: 301/251-5500.

National Institute for Sentencing Alternatives, 4-D Sydeman Hall, Brandeis University, Waltham, MA 02254. Phone: 617/893-4014.

Books

1. Victims

Bard, Morton, and Sangrey, Dawn. *The Crime Victim's Book*. New York: Basic Books, 1979.

Jackson, Dave. *Dial 911: Peaceful Christians and Urban Violence*. Scottdale, Pa.: Herald Press, 1981.

Schafer, Stephen. *Victimology: The Victim and His Criminal*. Reston, Va.: Reston Pub. Company, 1977.

Zehr, Howard. *Who Is My Neighbor? Learning to Care for Victims of Crime*. Elkhart, Ind.: Mennonite Central Committee, n.d.

Zehr, Howard. *The Christian as Victim*. Elkhart, Ind.: Mennonite Central Committee, n.d.

2. Prisoners

American Friends Service Committee. *Struggle for Justice*. New York: Hill and Wang, 1971.

Colson, Charles W. *Life Sentence*. Waco, Tex.: Chosen Books, 1979.

Goldfarb, Ronald L., and Singer, Linda R. *After Conviction*. New York: Simon and Schuster, 1973.

Irwin, John. *The Felon*. Englewood Cliffs, N.J.: Prentice-Hall, 1970.

Johnson, Robert, and Toch, Hans, eds. *The Pains of Imprisonment*. Beverly Hills: Sage Publications, 1982.

Keve, Paul W. *Prison Life and Human Worth*. Minneapolis: Univ. of Minnesota Press, 1974.

Mitford, Jessica. *Kind and Usual Punishment: The Prison Business*. New York: Alfred A. Knopf, 1973.

Shaw, George Bernard. *The Crime of Imprisonment*. New York: Philosophical Library, 1946.

Sykes, Gresham M. *The Society of Captives: A Study of a Maximum Security Prison*. Princeton: Princeton Univ. Press, 1958.

3. Historical and Philosophical Perspective

Berman, Harold J. *Law and Revolution: The Formation of the Western Legal Tradition*. Cambridge: Harvard Univ. Press, 1983.

Bottoms, A. E., and Preston, R. H., eds. *The Coming Penal Crisis: A Criminological and*

Theological Exploration. Edinburgh: Scottish Academic Press, 1980.

Christie, Nils. *Limits to Pain.* Oxford: Martin Robertson, 1981.

Elliston, Frederick, and Bowie, Norman, eds. *Ethics, Public Policy, and Criminal Justice.* Cambridge: Oelgeschlager, Gunn and Hain, 1982.

Forer, Lois G. *Criminals and Victims: A Trial Judge Reflects on Crime and Punishment.* New York: W. W. Norton, 1980.

Mackey, Virginia. *Punishment: In the Scripture and Tradition of Judaism, Christianity and Islam.* Rochester, N.Y.: National Inter-religious Task Force on Criminal Justice, 1981.

McKelvey, Blake. *American Prisons: A History of Good Intentions.* Montclair, N.J.: Patterson Smith, 1977.

Menninger, Karl. *The Crime of Punishment.* New York: Viking Press, 1966.

Rogers, Joseph W. *Why Are You Not a Criminal?* Englewood Cliffs, N.J.: Prentice-Hall, 1977.

Stott, John, and Miller, Nick, eds. *Crime and the Responsible Community.* Grand Rapids, Mich.: Eerdmans, 1980.

Von Hirsch, Andrew. *Doing Justice: The Choice of Punishments.* New York: Hill and Wang, 1976.

Wilson, James Q., and Herrnstein, Richard J. *Crime and Human Nature.* New York: Simon and Schuster, 1985.

Zehr, Howard. *Retributive Justice, Restorative Justice.* Elkhart, Ind.: Mennonite Central Committee, 1985.

4. Biblical Perspective

Birch, Bruce C., and Rasmussen, Larry L. *Bible and Ethics in the Christian Life.* Minneapolis: Augsburg, 1976.

Boecker, Hans Jochen, *Law and the Administration of Justice in the Old Testament and Ancient East.* Minneapolis: Augsburg, 1980.

Cotham, Perry C., ed. *Christian Social Ethics.* Grand Rapids, Mich.: Baker, 1979.

Haughey, John C., ed. *The Faith That Does Justice: Examining the Christian Sources for Social Change.* New York: Paulist Press, 1977.

Kaiser, Walter C. *Toward Old Testament Ethics.* Grand Rapids, Mich.: Zondervan, Academic Books, 1983.

Madigan, Kathleen E., and Sullivan, William J., eds. *Crime and Community in Biblical Perspective.* Valley Forge, Pa.: Judson Press, 1980.

Marshall, Paul. *Thine Is the Kingdom: A Biblical Perspective on the Nature of Government and Politics Today.* Basingstoke, Eng.: Marshalls, 1984.

McHugh, Gerald Austin. *Christian Faith and Criminal Justice: Toward a Christian Response to Crime and Punishment.* New York: Paulist Press, 1978.

Monsma, Stephen V. *Pursuing Justice in a Sinful World.* Grand Rapids, Mich.: Eerdmans, 1984.

Mott, Stephen Charles. *Biblical Ethics and Social Change.* New York: Oxford Univ. Press, 1982.

Payne, J. Barton. *The Theology of the Older Testament.* Grand Rapids, Mich.: Zondervan, 1962.

Rushdoony, Rousas John. *The Institutes of Biblical Law.* Nutley, N.J.: Presbyterian and Reformed, 1973.

Wolterstorff, Nicholas. *Until Justice and Peace Embrace.* Grand Rapids, Mich.: Eerdmans,

1983.
Wright, Christopher J. H. *An Eye for and Eye: The Place of Old Testament Ethics Today.* Downers Grove, Ill.: InterVarsity Press, 1983.

5. Reforms

Alper, Benedict S. *Prisons Inside-Out: Alternatives in Correctional Reform.* Cambridge: Ballinger, 1974.

Barnett, Randy E., and Hagel, John, III, eds. *Assessing the Criminal: Restitution, Retribution and the Legal Process.* Cambridge: Ballinger, 1977.

Campbell, Roger F. *Justice Through Restitution: Making Criminals Pay.* Milford, Mich.: Mott Media, 1977.

Galaway, Burt, and Hudson, Joe, eds. *Offender Restitution in Theory and Action.* Lexington, Mass.: Lexington Books, 1977.

Hudson, Joe, and Galaway, Burt, eds. *Victims, Offenders, and Alternative Sanctions.* Lexington, Mass.: Lexington Books, 1980.

Morris, Norval. *The Future of Imprisonment.* Chicago: Univ. of Chicago Press, 1974.

Skogan, Wesley G., and Maxfield, Michael G. *Coping with Crime: Individual and Neighborhood Reactions.* Beverly Hills: Sage Publications, 1981.

Solomon, Hassim. *Community Corrections.* Boston: Holbrook Press, 1976.

Sorrentino, Anthony. *Organizing Against Crime: Redeveloping the Neighborhood.* New York: Human Sciences Press, 1977.

Umbreit, Mark. *Crime and Reconciliation: Creative Options for Victims and Offenders.* Nashville, Tenn.: Abingdon Press, 1985.

Washnis, George, J. *Citizen Involvement in Crime Prevention.* Lexington, Mass.: Lexington Books, 1976.

Wright, Martin. *Making Good: Prisons, Punishment and Beyond.* London: Burnett Books, 1982.

Appendix B: How Much Restitution?

When restitution is ordered in Scripture, different amounts are required. In some instances, 500 per cent restitution is established (Ex 22:1); in others it is 400 per cent (Ex 22:1), 200 per cent (Ex 22:4, 7-9), 120 per cent (Lev 6:1-7), and 100 per cent (Ex 22:5-6, 10-15).

Why are the amounts different? A clue to the answer may be found in the provisions concerning personal injury. There restitution was not just for the amount of the medical bills, *but also for the lost time*. The Law recognized that there are losses other than out-of-pocket costs, such as lost wages. It has been suggested that the requirement of multiple restitution for theft was based on the recognition that the loss to the owner is greater than simply the market value of the stolen property:

> Multiple restitution rests on a principle of justice. Sheep are capable of a high rate of reproduction and have use, not only as meat, but also by means of their wool, for clothing, as well as other uses. To steal a sheep is to steal the present and future value of a man's property. The ox requires a higher rate of restitution, five-fold, because the ox was trained to pull carts, and to plow, and was used for a variety of farm tasks. The ox therefore had not only the value of its meat and its usefulness, but also the value of its training, in that training an ox for work was a task requiring time and skill. It thus commanded a higher rate of restitution. Clearly a principle of restitution is in evidence here. Restitution must calculate not only the present and future value of a thing stolen, but also the specialized skills involved in its replacement.[1]

In other words, the restitution ordered was in fact 100 per cent of the real loss to the victim, but happened, in different situations, to be multiple values of the actual purchase price of a replacement. A contemporary example might be that the theft of an antique vase could not be satisfied by simply buying a vase from a drug store. In one sense that would be restitution, since the victim would have a place to put flowers again, but no one would seriously argue that this would be fair compensation to the victim. Fair compensation might be many times more than the replacement cost.

The requirement of 120 per cent restitution in those cases in which the offender "turned himself in" apparently applied when the crime would have gone unsolved but for the confession. The amount of restitution was reduced as an incentive to the offender to make good his wrong.

There is another possible explanation for the different amounts of restitution: that it combines compensation with an additional charge for purposes of punishment. The reason there are differences in the amount is because the offenses involved degrees of culpability. For example, the offenses involving negligence (Ex 22:5-6, 10-15) resulted in only 100 per cent restitution. And in cases of theft, the amount of restitution was higher when the property had been destroyed (and hence could not be recovered) than when it was found in the possession of the thief.

But there are several problems with this explanation. First, the *lex talionis* established the principle that punishment must be proportionate to the wrong. Five oxen for one ox certainly violates the limitation of "an eye for an eye."

The second problem is that restitution for physical injury did not require multiple payment. The offender was to pay the cost of treating the victim and reimburse any lost wages. This simply restored the victim for out-of-pocket expenses. There was no additional amount for punishment purposes.

But why would personal injuries be treated less seriously than property loss? That would be the implication if multiple restitution was required for property offenses, but only simple restitution for violent offenses. This is particularly a problem because, as we saw in chapter 10, a characteristic of the Old Testament Law was that it valued people over property.

It is certainly possible to create a criminal justice system built on restitution and requiring multiple amounts for purposes of punishment. But the more satisfying explanation to me for the use of different amounts in Scripture is that the fundamental requirement was simple restitution, an eye for an eye. The casuistic format of the Exodus passages noted above suggests to me that these formulae arose out of specific cases in which the total value of property losses were determined.

Appendix C: Study Questions for Groups or Individuals

Chapter 1: Victims
1. Why did you decide to read this book? What do you hope to get out of it?
2. Have you ever been the victim of a crime? If so, how did you feel afterward?
3. What does Van Ness mean when he says that victims are just witnesses for the prosecution?
4. Do you think victims are justly compensated for their losses? How?
5. Do you think criminals are generally given appropriate punishments for their crimes? If not, in what ways do sentences tend to be inappropriate?
6. Why do you think that Christians ought to be concerned about crime?

Activity: Go to a local library and look up statistics on crime in your area. You could try to find, for example, the frequency of crime, the number of cases prosecuted, the rate of conviction, the types and duration of punishment.

Chapter 2: Being Victimized
1. Describe your own approach to crime: Do you feel fearful? Unconcerned? Secure? How have your feelings been different during different times of your life?
2. Van Ness says that sometimes we blame the victim for a crime. What does he mean? Do you think this actually happens?
3. Summarize the various stages victims go through in response to a crime.
4. Have you ever been called on to help someone who had been victimized? How did you respond? How would you respond based on Van Ness's advice?
5. Why can even a minor burglary, home invasion or vandalism be very upsetting? What is violated when your house is entered without your permission?
6. Describe your experience (or someone else's you know) in the court system. Did you feel you were treated fairly? Were you compensated in any way?

Activity: Find someone who was the victim of a crime for which an offender was caught and prosecuted. Ask them to describe the events and their feelings during (if applicable) and after the crime, during and after the trial, and since then.

Chapter 3: Prisoners
1. How did the story of Bradford Brown affect you? Have you ever heard a similar story?
2. As far as you know, were the conditions in Bradford Brown's prison unusually bad or fairly typical?
3. How do you think you would feel if you were sent to prison?
4. Did it surprise you to learn that most people sentenced to prison committed non-violent crimes? In your opinion, which nonviolent offenders should go to prison and which ones should not?
5. Why do you think it is that the United States puts a larger proportion of its population in prison than does any other country except South Africa and the Soviet Union?
6. Is sending a person to prison a good investment? How much does it cost and how often is the person rehabilitated?
Activity: Meet with the warden or a guard from a local prison. Talk to him or her about the conditions at the prison, the prisoners' responses to their situation, the number of offenders who return to prison after being released, and similar issues.
Or, read and discuss some of the books cited by Van Ness, such as Jeffrey Reimer's *The Rich Get Richer and the Poor Get Prison,* Philip Slater's *The Pursuit of Loneliness* or Gresham Sykes's *The Society of Captives,* or another book listed in Appendix A.

Chapter 4: Being Imprisoned
1. List and briefly describe the five earmarks of the prison experience.
2. If your local prison were like a Hilton Hotel, would you mind being sentenced to stay there for a year? Why or why not?
3. Would you mind living in a society that consisted of only men or only women? Why would that be strange?
4. What does Van Ness say happens to families when a member is in prison? What stresses do you think prison would put on families?
5. In what way does prison make prisoners dependent? That is, why might they have trouble adjusting to life outside prison?
6. What effect do you think overcrowding has on prisoners?
Activity: Discuss with the family of a prisoner the effect of imprisonment on that family. What are the emotional, financial and time costs? Who pays the most?
Or, contact the chaplain of a local prison and ask to speak to a prisoner. How does the prisoner feel about his or her experience? What has happened during the imprisonment? How is the prisoner's family doing? Does he or she receive much mail or visitors? Does he or she feel the imprisonment is a just punishment for the crime committed?

Chapter 5: The Rise of State-Centered Justice
1. Do you think the Old Testament penalty prescribed for the man who in anger injures another man was a just punishment? Why or why not?
2. What was the focus of ancient Middle Eastern and European laws? What was a typical punishment?
3. When did the focus of law change to an emphasis on violating the king's peace?
4. Why did that change take place?

5. When the focus of justice is on the state, what happens to the victim?

6. The original purpose of a state-centered justice system was to consolidate the power of the king. What purpose does it serve today in a democracy?

Activity: Make up an imaginary crime and describe how that crime might have been punished in ancient times and how it might be punished today.

Chapter 6: People vs. Defendant

1. After the development of a state-centered criminal justice system, why did the rights of accused persons need to be protected?

2. Describe some of the schools of criminology.

3. Do any of these schools of thought match your own beliefs about criminal behavior? Explain.

4. Why (if at all) were you surprised to learn that the first penitentary was begun by the Quakers at the end of the eighteenth century?

5. Can any conclusions be drawn from Van Ness's account of how our present prison system developed?

6. Each successive approach toward imprisonment seemed to recognize that the previous approach had failed and new thinking was needed. Do you believe that the time has again come for creative thinking about prisons? Explain your answer.

Activity: Invite a defense attorney and a public prosecutor to describe what legal protections are given to alleged criminals and what protections are provided for victims.

Or, think back on the theories about criminal behavior which Van Ness has presented. Try to formulate your own theory using what you know of psychology, sociology and the biblical view of human nature.

Chapter 7: The Purposes of Punishment

1. What are some of the factors that cause people to commit crimes? (Use Tom's story for an example and see also note #1.)

2. Explain why we punish criminals—what does the punishment signify and what are its purposes?

3. Can you think of any other purposes for punishment besides those listed by Van Ness?

4. Do you think that the threat of punishment deters criminals from committing crimes? Explain.

5. How are criminals supposed to be rehabilitated through punishment?

6. Did you think that Tom received a just sentence? Give the reasons for your response.

Activity: Think back to the punishments which were used on you as a child or which you have used with your own children. What kind of punishment seemed to encourage good behavior and which did not?

Or, invite a social worker who handles cases of juvenile delinquency to speak to your group. Ask this person to describe what conditions he or she thinks contribute to criminal behavior.

Chapter 8: The Mosaic Law

1. Why did God give the Law to the Israelites?

2. Describe the difficulties which arise when we try to apply the Old Testament Law

to our world.

3. According to Van Ness, what was Jesus' attitude toward the Law?

4. Why did Jesus' attitude upset the Pharisees?

5. Summarize the principles that Van Ness outlines to help us apply the Old Testament Law to contemporary situations.

6. Do you agree that the ethical demands of the Law were intended to be universal? Explain your answer.

Activity: Obtain a copy of your state's motor vehicle operator's manual (the book that each driver must learn before being licensed). That book contains a lot of very specific laws which apply to your particular state. But the specific laws are based on general principles about motor vehicle operation. Try to formulate some of those universal principles based on what you read in the manual.

Chapter 9: Justice and Righteousness

1. Describe in your own words the biblical concept of justice and righteousness.

2. Van Ness asserts that justice and righteousness bring about peace *(shalom)*. Describe what he means by peace.

3. What is the significance of the fact that the Israelite king was subject to the Law?

4. Is our president bound by law or is he above the law? Give examples of leaders who are not bound by the laws of their countries.

5. Van Ness points out that the legal process does not always bring about justice. Give examples (perhaps from the early chapters of the book) of how the legal process is divorced from the attempt to bring about justice.

6. Likewise, morality and legality are different things. Give examples of immoral acts which are legal or illegal acts which are moral.

Activity: Study Matthew 12:1-8. The passage reveals much about Jesus' attitude toward the Law. How does his attitude compare to that of the Pharisees? What was the most important thing in Jesus' eyes? What was most important to the Pharisees? Jesus quotes Hosea 6:6. This seems to summarize for him the purpose of the Law. What is it?

Or, read and discuss a key book on Old Testament Law, such as Walter Kaiser's *Toward Old Testament Ethics* or Christopher Wright's *An Eye for an Eye.*

Chapter 10: The Law and Criminal Justice

1. Give examples of religious, moral and civil laws from the Old Testament. Try also to think of contemporary civil laws which have religious and moral implications.

2. Summarize in your own words the general principles (pp. 129-32) which Van Ness draws out of the Old Testament.

3. Explain what restitution means. How was restitution provided for in the Old Testament? How has it been practiced down through the ages?

4. How (if at all) does restitution carry out the purposes of punishment—retribution, rehabilitation, deterrence and incapacitation?

5. Old Testament Law gives a lot of weight to the need for reconciliation between persons. What place does reconciliation have in our criminal justice system?

6. Given what you have read so far, do you think our current criminal justice system lives up to the biblical ideal? Where does it do so and where does it fall short?

Activity: Do a study of some of the key words relating to biblical ethics, such as *justice, righteousness, peace* or *reconciliation.* Use sources such as Colin Brown's *Dictionary of New Testament Theology,* George Arthur Buttrick's *The Interpreter's Dictionary of the Bible,* J. D. Douglas's *New Bible Dictionary,* and Gerhard Kittel's *Theological Dictionary of the New Testament.*

Chapter 11: Reducing Crime

1. Van Ness asserts that the present treatment of crime—as an offense against the state—may actually contribute to the frequency of crime. Why might this be the case?
2. Van Ness also relates crime to national values and investment in character building. Explain why you agree or disagree.
3. Have you ever been a part of a community crime prevention program? Describe your experience or tell what you know about programs available in your area. Why do you think neighborhood crime programs work?
4. Did it surprise you to learn that there appears to be a direct correlation between lack of religious commitment and crime? Why do you think this is so?
5. How do families and churches help to prevent crime?
6. Conservative Christians have tended to support the reintroduction of prayer into schools. But Van Ness speaks about a school curriculum which is not specifically religious yet which teaches basic moral values. What do you think of these curricula? Should Christians support them? What is the relationship between school prayer and the teaching of moral values?

Activity: Ask a policeman or community volunteer to talk to you about crime prevention programs in your community. Find out how they work and how effective they are.

Or, invite a member of your local public school board or a teacher to talk to you about values education. Is anything being done in your local schools? Do the teachers in your schools think that it is "off-limits" to teach values? Has your school board considered character education curricula?

Chapter 12: Responding to Crime

1. Explain the concept of restitution and how it is practiced. Why does it make sense to sentence a burglar or vandal to restitution rather than jail?
2. Explain how community service programs work. Are you familiar with any such programs?
3. What are the potential drawbacks to restitution or community service programs?
4. Are there any victim-offender mediation programs in your area? Why are such programs effective?
5. Does your state have programs which aid the victims of crime? Tell what you know about how they work.
6. Several states in the U.S. are beginning to sentence violent criminals to parole because there is no room for them in the prison system. Some such criminals have been "lost" in the parole system because parole officers are overloaded with cases. How would Van Ness's suggestions here alleviate this prison crisis?

Activity: Many states now have mandatory sentencing for certain types of criminals or for repeat offenders. For example, under Illinois law a person convicted more than three times for the nonviolent offense of burglary will receive a mandatory prison sentence of at least six years and up to thirty years without probation. Research what types of mandatory sentencing your state has or ask a criminal court judge to speak about such laws and give his or her views on them. In what ways do mandatory-sentencing laws aid the criminal justice process, and in what ways do they exacerbate the prison crisis?

Or, if there are special programs—such as restitution, community service, victim assistance or victim-offender reconciliation—in your area, invite someone to speak to you about how the programs work.

Chapter 13: Restraining Criminals

1. Besides prison, what means are available to incapacitate criminals and protect the public?

2. Do you think that first-time offenders and those who have committed nonviolent crimes should be in prison? Why or why not?

3. We have all heard of horrible cases where a paroled or early-released criminal has committed a terrible crime. Is this an argument against the reforms suggested by Van Ness? How would such cases be handled?

4. According to Van Ness, capital punishment is not prohibited by Scripture. Do you agree or disagree?

5. Under what circumstances, do you think, would it be biblically justifiable to sentence someone to death?

6. Very often the topic of criminal justice reform brings forth a heated debate over capital punishment. Should this be the focus of the discussion? How do you think that Christians who differ on capital punishment could work together for criminal justice reform?

Activity: Invite a parole officer to describe his or her job and the difficulties it presents. What sorts of prison or parole reforms would this person recommend? Do you agree or disagree?

Chapter 14: Where Do We Go from Here?

1. What is your response now that you have finished this book? Do you feel hopeful, discouraged, overwhelmed, enlightened, angry, bored, or something else?

2. How has your thinking changed as a result of your reading?

3. Why do you think that Ross Osborn's experience could or could not happen in your state?

4. Describe your experience, if any, with the various prison ministry and reform groups that are listed in this chapter.

5. Many people formulate their thinking and express their values in casual conversations. When you are talking to your friends and the subject of criminals or victims or prisons arises, how will your discussion be different now that you have read this book?

6. What will be your next step to take in response to the needs outlined here?

Activity: Numerous activites are recommended in this chapter. Let this be the beginning of your work on behalf of crime and its victims.

Notes

Chapter 1: Victims

[1]William W. Webster, *Crime in the United States, 1977* (Washington, D.C.: Government Printing Office, 1977), p. 23.

[2]Judge Lois Forer, who has had considerable experience with criminal trials, describes a shopkeeper who had been robbed three times: "The first two times her store had been held up she was so frightened that she could not even be sure of the clothing the robber was wearing, his height, or his weight." *Criminals and Victims: A Trial Judge Reflects on Crime and Punishment* (New York: W. W. Norton, 1980), p. 21.

[3]Elizabeth F. Loftus, *Eyewitness Testimony* (Cambridge, Mass.: Harvard Univ. Press, 1979), pp. 73-74, 144, 150-51.

[4]From a phone conversation on 9 January 1986 with Caroline Huntting of the National Organization for Victim Assistance. She told me that Simpson has continued to rally support, this time for legislative changes in the Youthful Offender Act. She has formed a task force to expose ways that the criminal justice system is unresponsive to the needs of victims. She is also helping set up a victim assistance program to provide practical help and support for victims of crime. (See chapter 11 for more information on victim assistance programs.)

Chapter 2: Being Victimized

[1]John Crothers Pollock, "Fear of Crime Changes Lives of Most Americans: Forty Percent Highly Fearful," *Criminal Justice Newsletter*, 11, no. 22 (10 November 1980): 2. This issue also contains a criticism of the report which questions the methodology of the researchers and therefore their conclusions. These criticisms are followed by the researchers' defense. Some of their conclusions appear to be overstated (for example, they said the country was paralyzed by fear). But their analysis of fear is helpful.

[2]Linda Heath, "Impact of Newspaper Crime Reports on Fear of Crime: Multimethodological Investigation," *Journal of Personality and Social Psychology* 47 (2): 263.

[3]Paul Lavrakas et al., "Fear of Crime and the Figgie Report: America Misrepresented,"

Criminal Justice Newsletter 11, no. 22 (10 November 1980): 4.

[4]Michael Rand, *Households Touched by Crime, 1983* (Washington, D.C.: Bureau of Justice Statistics, 1984), p. 1.

[5]Stephen Schafer, *Victimology: The Victim and His Criminal* (Reston, Va.: Reston Pub. Co., 1968), p. 34.

[6]Ibid., pp. 45-46.

[7]Benjamin Mendelsohn, quoted in Schafer, *Victimology*, p. 35.

[8]Michael R. Rand et al., "The Criminal Event," in *Report to the Nation*, ed. Zawitz, p. 2.

[9]"Researchers have used a number of different definitions of victim precipitation: studies in this area present all sorts of methodological problems. However, the work that has been done indicates that perhaps 26% of homicide cases involve victims who precipitated the crime; 19% of rape cases may involve such victims; 14% of aggravated assaults, and 11% of robberies." Morton Bard and Dawn Sangrey, *The Crime Victim's Book* (New York: Basic Books, 1979), p. 75, n. 5.

[10]Klaus et al., "The Victim," in *Report to the Nation on Crime and Justice: the Data*, ed. Marianne W. Zawitz (Washington, D.C.: Department of Justice, 1983), p. 20.

[11]For example: Bard and Sangrey, *The Crime Victim's Book;* David Jackson, *DIAL 911: Peaceful Christians and Urban Violence* (Scottdale, Pa.: Herald Press, 1981); and two booklets by Howard Zehr, "Who Is My Neighbor?" and "The Christian as Victim" (Mennonite Central Committee Office of Criminal Justice, 115 West Cleveland, Elkhart, IN 46516).

[12]Bard and Sangrey, *The Crime Victim's Book*, pp. 28ff.

[13]Ibid., p. 44.

[14]Zehr, "Who Is My Neighbor?" p. 11.

[15]Ibid.

[16]Ibid., p. 4.

[17]Bard and Sangrey, *The Crime Victim's Book*, p. 47.

[18]Zehr, "Who Is My Neighbor?" p. 9.

[19]Bard and Sangrey, *The Crime Victim's Book*, p. 46.

[20]From a phone conversation with Caroline Huntting of the National Organization for Victim Assistance on 9 January 1986.

[21]Karl Menninger, *The Crime of Punishment* (New York: Viking Press, 1966), p. 276.

Gerald Kaufman, director of the National Prison Overcrowding Project cited a study in the *Los Angeles Times*, 26 December 1983, which found that of 800,000 crimes committed in Colorado, 400,000 were reported, 25,000 people were arrested, 13,000 offenders were convicted, 3,000 were imprisoned.

[22]See Schafer, *Victimology*, pp. 107 ff., for an overview of compensation programs in the United States and other countries.

[23]J. Frederick Shenk and Patsy A. Klaus, *The Economic Cost of Crime to Victims* (Washington D.C.: Bureau of Justice Statistics, 1984), p. 3.

[24]Bard and Sangrey, *The Crime Victim's Book*, p. 18.

Chapter 3: Prisoners

[1]*Bradford G. Brown v. District of Columbia*, Civil Action No. 11595-81 (D.C. 11 July 1985) (Memorandum order). See also Elsa Walsh, "DC Court Compensates Jailed Man,"

Washington Post, 12 July 1985.
[2]Urbina (Memorandum order), p. 16.
[3]Ibid., p. 23, emphasis his.
[4]Allen J. Beck and Lawrence A. Greenfeld, *Prisoners in 1984* (Washington D.C.: Bureau of Justice Statistics, 1985), p. 4.
[5]Charles W. Colson, "Toward an Understanding of Imprisonment and Rehabilitation," *Crime and the Responsible Community*, ed. John Stott and Nick Miller (Grand Rapids, Eerdmans, 1980), pp. 165-66.
[6]Jeffrey H. Reimer, *The Rich Get Richer and the Poor Get Prison* (New York: John Wiley and Son, 1979).
[7]George Camp and Camille Camp, *The Corrections Yearbook* (South Salem N.Y.: Criminal Justice Institute, Inc., 1984), pp. 12-13.
[8]Philip E. Slater, *The Pursuit of Loneliness: American Culture at the Breaking Point* (Boston: Beacon Press, 1976), p. 21.
[9]According to the United States Census Bureau, the United States population grew 11 per cent from 215,973,000 on July 1, 1975, to 238,816,000 on July 1, 1985. Bureau of Justice Statistics data show that the prison population grew 113 per cent, from 218,205 on January 1, 1975, to 463,866 on January 1, 1985.
[10]Hana Umlauf Lane, ed., *The World Almanac and Book of Facts: 1985* (New York: Newspaper Enterprise Association, 1984), pp. 247, 263, 280, 515-600.
[11]Eugene Doleschal and Anne Newton, "International Rates of Imprisonment," mimeographed (Hackensack, N.J.: National Council on Crime and Delinquency, 1981).
[12]Clarence M. Kelley, *Crime in the United States: 1975* (Washington, D.C.: Government Printing Office, 1975), p. 44.
[13]Warren E. Burger, quoted in "Ex-Prisoners Can Become Producers, Not Predators," *Nation's Business* (October 1983): 39.
[14]Anthony Travisono, "There Are Time Bombs Ticking Away in Our Prisons and Jails," *Corrections Digest* (17 July 1981): 1.
[15]George Camp and Camille Camp, *The Corrections Yearbook* (South Salem, N.Y.: Criminal Justice Institute, 1985), p. 26.
[16]The 1985-86 tuition, room and board costs at Harvard were $15,100 and at Yale were $15,020. Andrea E. Lehmann, ed., *Guide to Four-Year Colleges: 1986* (Princeton: Peterson's Guides, 1985), pp. 1261, 2197. Tuition, room and board at state colleges averaged $4,600 for 1983-84. *Washington Post*, 11 July 1983.
[17]"Estimated 30-Year Life Cycle Cost for a Correctional Agency" (Chicago: Moyer Associates, 1981).
[18]Diana N. Travisono, ed., *1985 Juvenile and Adult Correctional Departments, Institutions, Agencies and Paroling Authorities Directory* (College Park, Md.: American Correctional Association, 1985), pp. x-xi.

Chapter 4: Being Imprisoned

[1]From James B. Finley, *Memorials of Prison Life*, quoted in David J. Rothman, "The Invention of the Penitentiary," *Criminal Law Bulletin* 8, no. 7 (1972): 561.
[2]Gresham M. Sykes, *The Society of Captives: A Study of a Maximum Security Prison* (Princeton, N.J.: Princeton Univ. Press, 1971), pp. 63ff. The prison he studied was the New Jersey State Prison in Trenton.

[3]George Bernard Shaw, *The Crime of Imprisonment* (New York: Philosophical Library, 1946), p. 21.

[4]Beck and Greenfeld, *Prisoners in 1984,* p. 4.

[5]Sidney Friedman and T. Conway Esselstyn, "The Adjustment of Children of Jail Inmates," *Federal Probation* 29, no. 4 (1965): 55-59.

[6]Sykes, *Society of Captives,* p. 66.

[7]Charles W. Colson, *Born Again* (New York: Bantam Books, 1976), p. 303.

[8]David Rohm, "Improvements Ordered for State Reformatory," *Indianapolis News,* 7 May 1982.

[9]Sykes, *Society of Captives,* p. 72.

[10]Laura J. Bakker et al., "Hidden Victims of Crime," *Social Work* 23, no. 2 (1978): 143-48; David P. Schneller, "Some Social and Psychological Effects of Incarceration on the Families of Negro Prisoners," *American Journal of Correction* 37, no. 1 (1975): 29-33.

[11]Michael A. Heymann, "The Hidden Costs of Life in Prison," *New York Times,* 7 January 1982.

[12]David Rudovsky, "Criminal Justice: The Accused," in *Our Endangered Rights,* ed. Norman Dorsen (New York: Pantheon Books, 1984), p. 223.

[13]John Irwin, *The Felon* (Englewood Cliffs, N.J.: Prentice-Hall, 1970), p. 125.

[14]Urbina (Memorandum order), p. 17.

[15]Steve Lerner, "Role of the Cruel: How Violence Is Built into America's Prisons," *The New Republic* (15 October 1984): 19.

[16]*Washington Star,* 29 October 1977.

[17]Joan Mullen, *American Prisons and Jails,* vol. 1 (Washington, D.C.: Government Printing Office, 1980), p. 61.

[18]*The Effect of Prison Crowding on Inmate Behavior* (Washington, D.C.: Government Printing Office, 1980).

[19]See David Farrington, "Prison Size, Overcrowding, Prison Violence and Recidivism," *Journal of Criminal Justice* 8 (1980); Lee-Jan Jan, "Overcrowding and Inmate Behavior," *Criminal Justice and Behavior* 7 (1980); and Nacci, Teitelbaum and Prather, "Population Density and Inmate Misconduct Rates in the Federal Prison System," *Federal Probation* (1977): 26.

[20]Griffin Bell and James Thompson, *Final Report: Attorney General's Task Force on Violent Crime* (Washington, D.C.: Government Printing Office, 1981), p. 10.

[21]Laura Mecoy, "Cost of Ending Overcrowding of Prisons Is Prohibitive," *Los Angeles Daily News,* 25 December 1983.

[22]Warren E. Burger, "Annual Report to the American Bar Association," an address delivered in Houston, Texas, on 8 February 1981.

Chapter 5: The Rise of State-Centered Justice

[1]Marvin E. Wolfgang describes early Western social structures as "familistic, involuntary, primary, sacred, traditional, emotional and personal. In contrast, contemporary society and law are built largely upon a . . . system characterized by social interaction that is voluntary, secular, secondary, rationalistic, and impersonal." "Victim Compensation in Crimes of Personal Violence," *Minnesota Law Review* 50 (1965): 223.

[2]Hammurabi, Law 8, trans. Theophile J. Meek, in James B. Pritchard, ed., *The Ancient*

Near East, vol. 1, *An Anthology of Texts and Pictures* (Princeton: Princeton Univ. Press, 1958), p. 140.

³Hans Jochen Boecker, *Law and the Administration of Justice in the Old Testament and Ancient East,* trans. Jeremy Moiser (Minneapolis: Augsburg, 1980), pp. 57-58.

⁴Ibid., pp. 58-60.

⁵Eshnunna, Laws 42-47, trans. Albrecht Goetze, in Pritchard, *The Ancient Near East,* p. 137.

⁶Schafer, *Victimology,* pp. 9-10.

⁷Tacitus, *Germania,* chapter 21, cited by Schafer, *Victimology,* p. 11.

⁸*Lex Salica,* ed. and trans. Ernest F. Henderson, *Select Historical Documents of the Middle Ages,* cited in Harold Berman, *Law and Revolution: The Formation of the Western Legal Tradition* (Cambridge, Mass.: Harvard Univ. Press, 1983), p. 52.

⁹Laws of Ethelbert in *The Laws of the Earliest English Kings,* trans. F. L. Attenborough, cited in Berman, *Law and Revolution,* p. 54.

¹⁰"The job is to clean the case up, to suppress or penalize the illegal behavior and to bring the relations of the disputants back into balance, so that life may resume its normal course. This type of law-work has frequently been compared to work of the medical practitioner. It is family doctor stuff, essential to keeping the social body on its feet." E. Adamson Hoebel, *The Law of Primitive Man: A Study in Comparative Legal Dynamics* (New York: Atheneum, 1973), p. 279.

¹¹Frank Barlow, "The Effects of the Norman Conquest" in Dorothy Whitelock et al., *The Norman Conquest: Its Setting and Impact* (New York: Scribner's, 1966), pp. 133-36.

¹²Berman, *Law and Revolution,* pp. 53-54.

¹³The struggle between the church and secular authorities continued for centuries. It was sometimes a violent conflict. It was the courtiers of King Henry II, for example, the great-grandson of William the Conqueror, who murdered Thomas à Becket, the archbishop of Canterbury, because he refused to give the king control over the ecclesiastical courts. By the sixteenth century, the kings in England and throughout Europe had successfully asserted control over civil and criminal law (although in England this was done simply by giving the king control of the church courts). Ibid., pp. 255-56.

¹⁴This excerpt from the *Leges Henrici* is quoted in A. C. Germann, Frank B. Day and Robert R. J. Gallati, *Introduction to Law Enforcement and Criminal Justice* (Springfield, Ill.: Charles C. Thomas, 1978), p. 50.

¹⁵Patrick D. McAnany, "Restitution as Idea and Practice" in *Offender Restitution in Theory and Action,* ed. Burt Galaway and Joe Hudson (Lexington, Mass.: Lexington Books, 1978), p. 17.

¹⁶Berman, *Law and Revolution,* p. 314.

¹⁷"As the state monopolized the institution of punishment, the rights of the injured were slowly separated from the penal law: composition, as the obligation to pay damages, became separated from criminal law and became a special field in civil law." Schafer, *Victimology,* p. 14.

¹⁸Schafer, *Victimology,* p. 5.

Chapter 6: People vs. Defendant

¹Zehr, "Who Is My Neighbor?" p. 6.

[2]Quoted in T. Walter Wallbank et al., *Civilization Past and Present* (Glenview, Ill.: Scott, Foresman, 1967), pp. 207-8.

[3]Germann et al., *Introduction to Law Enforcement*, p. 56.

[4]Wallbank et al., *Civilization Past and Present*, p. 427.

[5]Of course, there were theories before that time concerning why people committed transgressions. For a helpful overview of the changing notion of sin and sinners in the Christian church, see Gerald Austin McHugh, *Christian Faith and Criminal Justice: Toward a Christian Response to Crime and Punishment* (New York: Paulist Press, 1978), pp. 11ff.

[6]Cesare Beccaria, *On Crimes and Punishment* (1764), trans. Henry Paolucci (New York: Bobbs-Merrill, 1963). Jeremy Bentham, *An Introduction to the Principles of Morals and Legislation* (1789), ed. W. Harrison (Oxford: Basil Blackwell, 1948).

[7]Hassim M. Solomon, *Community Corrections* (Boston: Holbrook Press, 1976), p. 17.

[8]Ronald C. Kramer, "The Debate Over the Definition of Crime: Paradigms, Value Judgments, and Criminological Work," in *Ethics, Public Policy and Criminal Justice*, ed. Frederick Elliston and Norman Bowie (Cambridge, Mass.: Oegleschlager, Gunn and Hin, 1982), p. 35.

[9]Don C. Gibbons, *Society, Crime and Criminal Behavior* (Englewood Cliffs, N.J.: Prentice-Hall, Inc., 1982), p. 17.

[10]Cesare Beccaria, quoted in David J. Rothman, "Sentencing Reforms in Historical Perspective," *Crime and Delinquency* (October 1983): 632.

[11]Ibid.

[12]Solomon, *Community Corrections*, p. 18.

[13]Kramer, "The Debate Over the Definition of Crime," p. 35.

[14]Gibbons, *Society, Crime, and Criminal Behavior*, pp. 20-21.

[15]James Q. Wilson and Richard J. Herrnstein, *Crime and Human Nature* (New York: Simon and Schuster, 1985).

[16]Kramer, "The Debate Over the Definition of Crime," p. 36.

[17]Ibid., pp. 33ff.

[18]In a fascinating article in 1975, criminologist Paul Takagi argued that the drive to centralize the powers of the state (which we have seen was a major impetus to the creation of "criminal law") was a key factor in Pennsylvania's adoption of the Quaker notion of the penitentiary as a form of punishment.

The Walnut Street Jail, as a state prison, came into existence when penal powers came to be monopolized by the State. The significance of a state prison and the adoption of the model in New York in 1796 and by other states, was not so much the architectural design and the classification of prisoners, but the concept of a centralized state apparatus. Here, the issue is not the level of government operations, that is to say a state versus a county operated prison; it has to do with the establishment of a special public force with powers to exact revenue, to appoint officials with special privileges and power, and the right to use force to whatever degree is necessary. (Paul Takagi, "The Walnut Street Jail: A Penal Reform to Centralize the Powers of the State," *Federal Probation* (December 1975): 24.

[19]McHugh, *Christian Faith and Criminal Justice*, pp. 20-21.

[20]Ronald C. Goldfarb and Linda R. Singer, *After Conviction* (New York: Simon and Schuster, 1973), pp. 20-21.

[21]"Imprisonment is mentioned in only one late text (Ezra 7:26), but the reference here is to a practice commanded by Artaxerxes." Boecker, *Law and the Administration of Justice*, p. 133.

[22]Francis T. Cullen and Karen E. Gilbert, *Reaffirming Rehabilitation* (Cincinnati: Anderson Publishing, 1982), pp. 46-51.

[23]Ibid., pp. 49-50.

[24]McHugh, *Christian Faith and Criminal Justice*, p. 35.

[25]Goldfarb and Singer, *After Conviction*, p. 23.

[26]Quoted in ibid., p. 26.

[27]Ibid., p. 37.

[28]Rothman, "Invention of the Penitentiary," p. 567.

[29]Blake McKelvey, *American Prisons: A History of Good Intentions* (Montclair, N.J.: Patterson Smith, 1977), pp. 9, 14.

[30]McHugh, *Christian Faith and Criminal Justice*, pp. 39-40.

[31]McKelvey, *American Prisons*, p. 15.

[32]The prisons at Auburn, Wethersfield, Charlestown and Baltimore actually made a profit. Ibid., p. 21.

[33]Ibid., pp. 49-50.

[34]Philip Jenkins, "Temperance and the Origins of the New Penology," *Journal of Criminal Justice* 12 (1984): 560.

[35]McKelvey, *American Prisons*, pp. 69-70.

[36]Ibid., p. 90.

[37]Ibid., pp. 137-38.

[38]Goldfarb and Singer, *After Conviction*, p. 42.

[39]McKelvey, *American Prisons*, pp. 138-39.

[40]McHugh, *Christian Faith and Criminal Justice*, p. 51.

[41]Ibid., p. 53.

[42]Statement made at Prison Fellowship Leadership Conference, Washington, D.C., 19 September 1980.

[43]Andrew von Hirsch et al., *Doing Justice: The Choice of Punishments* (New York: Hill and Wang, 1976).

Chapter 7: The Purposes of Punishment

[1]Harry Elmer Barnes and Negley K. Teeters describe these categories in *New Horizons in Criminology* (Englewood Cliffs, N.J.: Prentice-Hall, 1959), pp. 116-210. See also Edwin H. Sutherland and Donald R. Cressey, *Criminology* (Philadelphia: Lippincott, 1970), pp. 48-70.

1. *Constitutional.* While the early claim of Lombroso that there are "born criminals" has few adherents, there continue to be studies exploring physical factors that may lead people to crime. Among these are ones focusing on endocrinology (the study of ductless glands), genetics, body build (endomorphic, mesomorphic and ectomorphic body types behave differently), mental retardation, nutrition and so forth.

2. *Geographical.* These theorists have studied the effects of the offender's environment, including urban and rural differences, and seasonal or climate-related crime rate variations.

3. *Economic.* Research has documented that a disproportionate number of poor

people are arrested, convicted and imprisoned. Explanations have ranged from a form of economic determinism which says that poor people commit crimes because it is the only way to survive, to a political theory which says that criminal laws focus on the behavior poor people are more likely to engage in and ignore the wrongful acts the rich are likely to commit.

4. *Sociologic.* Most courses in criminology are taught in sociology classes and most of the textbooks are written by sociologists. Perhaps this is why sociological explanations for crime are best known. These focus on the community and its effect on the individual living in it. They have addressed criminal subcultures, home and family situations, and the behavior of minorities living in a dominant culture.

5. *Psychiatric.* Many view criminal behavior as stemming from an inability to face reality and the resulting mental conflicts. The offender is "sick" and in need of treatment.

[2]Barnes and Teeters, *New Horizons,* pp. 207-8.

[3]Samuel Yochelson and Stanton Samenow, *The Criminal Personality* (New York: J. Aronsun, 1977).

[4]David Lovell, "Punishment," mimeographed, Connecticut Department of Correction (340 Capitol Avenue, Hartford, Conn.), p. 8.

[5]These are derived from "Punishment," an article written by David Lovell, a philosopher who was hired by the Connecticut Department of Correction to work with them for one year to think and write about punishment.

[6]Nils Christie, *Limits to Pain* (Oxford: Martin Robertson, 1981), p. 94. Christie contrasts the values clarification that comes from degrees of punishment with what he believes would be the same clarification coming from what he calls "participatory justice" in which conflict is not so much *solved* by the criminal justice system as it is *handled* through the involvement of all the parties. But as long as that "handling" is enforced by the government, and as long as there are any punitive aspects to the resolution, his recommendations relate more to the method by which the sanctions are determined than to the form of the sanctions.

[7]Joel Feinberg states these purposes somewhat differently: (1) *authoritative disavowal* in which those in authority condemn the behavior of those who violate the law; (2) *symbolic nonacquiesence* in which society separates itself from the criminal behavior of the individual; (3) *vindication of the law* in which the written law is upheld; and (4) *absolution of others* in which punishment of certain suspects clears those not punished from blame. Joel Feinberg, *Doing and Deserving: Essays in the Theory of Responsibility* (Princeton: Princeton Univ. Press, 1970), pp. 101-5.

[8]Charles W. Colson, "Towards an Understanding of the Origins of Crime," in *Crime and the Responsible Community,* ed. Stott and Miller, p. 37.

[9]Alfred Blumstein et al., eds., *Deterrence and Incapacitation: Estimating the Effects of Criminal Sanctions on Crime Rates* (Washington, D.C.: National Academy of Sciences, 1978).

[10]William H. Webster, *Crime in the United States, 1984* (Washington, D.C.: Government Printing Office, 1984), pp. 6-12.

[11]Kenneth Carlson, *Mandatory Sentencing: The Experience of Two States* (Washington, D.C.: National Institute of Justice, 1982), p. 6.

[12]Germann, *Introduction to Law Enforcement,* p. 58.

[13]Deut 17:13 concerns someone who deliberately refuses to obey a court judgment; Deut

19:19 concerns someone who brings false witness against another in a judicial proceeding; Deut 13:11 concerns someone who urges others to worship gods other than Jehovah.

[14]Robert Martinson, "What Works? Questions and Answers about Prison Reform," *Public Interest,* Spring 1974, pp. 22-54.

[15]Paul Gendreau and Robert Ross, "Offender Rehabilitation: The Appeal of Success," *Federal Probation,* December 1981, p. 46.

[16]Ibid., p. 45.

[17]For example, Orsagh and Marsden have applied the rational-choice theory in economics to rehabilitation of offenders and have hypothesized that this is why economically motivated offenders respond positively to income-enhancing programs such as skills training. Thomas Orsagh and Mary Ellen Marsden, "What Works When: Rational-Choice Theory and Offender Rehabilitation," *Journal of Criminal Justice* 13 (1985): 269-77.

[18]C. S. Lewis, "The Humanitarian Theory of Punishment," in *God in the Dock: Essays on Theology and Ethics,* ed. Walter Hooper (Grand Rapids, Mich.: Eerdmans, 1970), pp. 287-300.

[19]Cullen and Gilbert, *Reaffirming Rehabilitation,* p. 246.

[20]Von Hirsch et al., *Doing Justice,* p. 19.

[21]Peter W. Greenwood, "Selective Incapacitation: A Method of Using Our Prisons More Effectively," *NIJ Reports* (January 1984): 6.

[22]Thomas J. Reese, "Demythologizing Crime," *America,* 24 March 1984, p. 215.

[23]Jacqueline Cohen, "Incapacitating Criminals: Recent Research Findings," *NIJ Research in Brief* (December 1983): 4.

[24]As of January 1983, thirty states had enacted such laws. Jim Galvin, "Setting Prison Terms" (Washington, D.C.: Bureau of Justice Statistics, 1983), p. 3.

[25]Cohen, "Incapacitating Criminals," p. 3.

Chapter 8: The Mosaic Law

[1]Gordon D. Fee and Douglas Stuart, *How to Read the Bible for All Its Worth* (Grand Rapids, Mich.: Zondervan, 1982), p. 136.

[2]Walter C. Kaiser, Jr., *Toward Old Testament Ethics* (Grand Rapids, Mich.: Zondervan, 1983), pp. 42ff.

[3]See, for example, Fee and Stuart, *How to Read the Bible,* p. 139.

[4]This is an adaptation of steps outlined in John Goldingay, *Approaches to Old Testament Interpretation* cited in Kaiser, *Toward Old Testament Ethics,* p. 43. See also, Bruce C. Birch and Larry L. Rasmussen, *Bible and Ethics in the Christian Life* (Minneapolis: Augsburg, 1976), pp. 161ff.

[5]So while Christians are certainly no longer "under the law" (Rom 3:19; 6:14), i.e., bound by the law of the old covenant, they are nevertheless not "without the law" (1 Cor 9:21), as though it had nothing whatever to say to them. Rather, the power of the indwelling Spirit makes it possible "that the righteous requirements of the law might be fully met in us who . . . live . . . according to the Spirit" (Rom 8:4). Christopher J. H. Wright, *An Eye for an Eye: The Place of Old Testament Ethics Today* (Downers Grove, Ill.: InterVarsity Press, 1983), p. 160.

[6]Lewis Smedes, *Mere Morality* (Grand Rapids, Mich.: Eerdmans, 1983), p. 10.

Chapter 9: Justice and Righteousness
[1]"The standard for the good, the right, the just, and the acceptable is nothing less than the person of the living God: 'Be holy *because* I, the Lord your God, am holy' " (Lev 19:2). Wright, *Eye for an Eye*, p. 6 (emphasis added).
[2]"This close connection between ethics and theology constitutes one of the distinctive features of the Bible's own set of ethics. Accordingly, what God is in his character, and what he wills in his revelation, defines what is right; conversely it is right, good, acceptable, and satisfying to all because of his known character and will." Kaiser, *Toward Old Testament Ethics*, p. 3.
[3]"We must bear in mind that the Old Testament nowhere refers to legislation on the part of the king. The laws of the Old Testament were not promulgated by the king and therefore not by the state either. They were given by God. Jahweh, the God of Israel, was the sole legislator. This was essentially different from other ancient eastern countries. Although Hammurabi for example acted by divine commission, it was as king of Babylon that he wrote his code and expressly described himself as lawgiver." Hans Jochen Boecker, *Law and the Administration of Justice in the Old Testament and Ancient East* (Minneapolis: Augsburg, 1980), p. 41.
[4]Theologian R. C. Sproul has written a very helpful book on the holiness of God which argues that regardless of how draconian the punishments which God imposed on those who violated his commands appear to us, they were actually just and appropriate. He contends that they appear unfair only because we do not understand the biblical concepts of *holiness, justice, sin,* and *grace*. R. C. Sproul, *The Holiness of God* (Wheaton, Ill.: Tyndale, 1985), pp. 129-68.
[5]"Yahweh's justice is saving justice where punishment of the sinner is an integral part of salvation." John R. Donahue, S.J., ed., *The Faith That Does Justice: Examining the Christian Sources for Social Change*, ed. John C. Haughey, S.J. (New York: Paulist Press, 1977), p. 72.
[6]J. Barton Payne, "Justice," *New Bible Dictionary*, 2nd ed., ed. J. D. Douglas (Wheaton, Ill.: Tyndale, 1982), p. 645.
[7]An excellent introduction to these words is found in Wright, *Eye for an Eye*, pp. 133ff.
[8]J. Barton Payne, *The Theology of the Older Testament* (Grand Rapids, Mich.: Zondervan, 1962), p. 156.
[9]Harold G. Stigers, *"Sadeq,"* in *Theological Wordbook of the Old Testament*, ed. R. Laird Harris et al. (Chicago: Moody Press, 1980), p. 752.
[10]Wright, *Eye for an Eye*, p. 134.
[11]The word *tseaqah* is "used frequently throughout the Old Testament for the cry, complaint or appeal of one who is suffering injustice. It is the word used to describe the cry of the poor and needy which resulted in the destruction of Sodom and Gomorrah. It is the cry of Israel in their slavery in Egypt. This word 'outcry' is also a technical legal term. It is an appeal to the courts to rectify injustice." Paul Marshall, *Thine Is the Kingdom: A Biblical Perspective on the Nature of Government and Politics Today* (Basingstoke, Eng.: Marshalls, 1984), p. 39.
[12]Gottfried Quell and Gottlob Schrenk, "Righteousness," in *Manuals from Kittel*, Gerhard Kittel (London: Adam and Charles Black, 1951), p. 3.
[13]G. Lloyd Carr, *"Shalom,"* in *Theological Wordbook*, Harris, p. 930.
[14]Ibid., p. 931.

[15]I am indebted to Walter Klaassen for this illustration. He uses it to draw provocative categories of responses to injustice, in a monograph published by the Mennonite Central Committee of Canada Victim Offender Ministries in 1985, entitled "Peoplehood and Law."

[16]Carl F. H. Henry, *God, Revelation and Authority*, vol. 6, *God Who Stands and Stays* (Waco, Tex.: Word Books, 1983), pp. 418-19.

[17]Lawrence Kohlberg, "Moral Judgment Interview and Procedures for Scoring," cited in Madigan and Sullivan, *Crime and Community in Biblical Perspective* (Valley Forge, Pa.: Judson Press, 1980), p. 49.

[18]"The great fault of contemporary civilization lies not in the public's disposition to overestimate the importance of law, but rather to underestimate it; many evangelical Christians share that error." Henry, *God, Revelation and Authority*, p. 435.

[19]Paul B. Henry, "Christian Perspectives on Power Politics," in *Christian Social Ethics*, ed. Perry C. Cotham (Grand Rapids, Mich.: Baker, 1979), p. 74.

Chapter 10: The Law and Criminal Justice

[1]Although the many commandments are scattered throughout the different narrative settings of Exodus, Leviticus, Numbers and Deuteronomy, there are also concentrations or clusters of commandments. Best known, of course, is the Ten Commandments (Ex 20:2-17; Deut 5:6-21), which in Exodus is part of a longer section called the "Book of the Covenant" (Ex 20:2—23:33). There is also the "Holiness Code" (Lev 1—7), so called because it deals with the laws concerning how the nation was to conduct its worship. Numbers, the book of Israel's wilderness wanderings, also contains clusters of commands (5:1—10:10; 15; 28—30). And Deuteronomy, a series of sermons on the Law preached by Moses just before they entered the Land, is a repetition (the word means "second law") and commentary on the provisions in Exodus, Leviticus and Numbers.

[2]Fee and Stuart, *How to Read the Bible*, p. 146.

There is an additional distinction which Old Testament scholars have noted: the laws themselves are written in different forms. Some of them are written as absolutes and directly command or prohibit certain behavior. They often begin "Thou shalt" or "Thou shalt not." The Ten Commandments are an example of this kind of form, which Bible scholars call *apodictic* laws.

The second basic format is case-by-case law. You will recognize this in laws that begin with *if* and end with *then*. They refer to specific instances and explain how the people were to make judgments under those conditions. These kind of laws are called *casuistic* laws. And because they show how a specific case would be resolved, they gave the people guidance in deciding other kinds of cases which were similar, but not identical.

Case law is a fundamental part of American law, derived from the English law we adopted when our nation was formed. Judges decide individual cases by applying principles of law to a specific factual situation. But by making that decision, they also help shape the meaning of the principle itself, since their cases offer guidance to other judges considering similar cases in the future.

That is what casuistic law did. It set out a specific problem and then said how that should be resolved. The job of those who were to judge in disputes was to apply the underlying principle to the specific case. Fee and Stuart, *How to Read the Bible*, pp. 139-44.

It is important to remember that casuistic law is just as much a part of the Law as the apodictic law, in the same way that United States Supreme Court decisions are just as much law as the legislation that is passed by Congress.

[3]Wright, *Eye for an Eye*, p. 162.

[4]Boecker, *Law and the Administration of Justice*, pp. 171-75.

[5]Ibid., p. 166.

[6]"If a seignior made a breach in a house, they shall put him to death in front of that breach and wall him in." Hammurabi, Law 21, in Pritchard, *Ancient Near East*, p. 141.

[7]Eshnunna, Laws 23 and 24, in Pritchard, *Ancient Near East*, p. 135.

[8]Hammurabi, Laws 209-14, in Pritchard, *Ancient Near East*, p. 162.

[9]See also, N. H. Ridderbos, "Cities of Refuge," *New Bible Dictionary*, p. 234.

[10]Examples of judgment include the stoning of Achan and his family for disobeying God's directive that no plunder be taken from Jericho (Josh 7), and the destruction of Ananias and Sapphira for lying about giving all the proceeds of the sale of property to the early church (Acts 5:1-11). Examples of grace include the forgiveness and restoration of David (2 Sam 12:13-14) and of Peter (Jn 18:15-18; 25-27; 21:15-17).

[11]For a complete list of the offenses punishable by death, see Rousas John Rushdoony, *The Institutes of Biblical Law* (Nutley, N.J.: Presbyterian and Reformed, 1973), p. 235.

[12]The first (and only) mention in Scripture of prisons used to punish guilty criminals is found in Ezra 7:26. This is part of Artaxerxes' proclamation, and therefore refers to Persian, not biblical, law. Rushdooney, *Institutes of Biblical Law*, pp. 514-15.

[13]Augustine, in the fourth century after Christ, wrote:

> If the offense committed has involved theft, and restitution is not made, although it is possible to make it, there is no repentance but only pretense. If, however, there is true repentance, the sin will not be forgiven unless there is restitution of stolen goods. (*St. Augustine's Letters, The Fathers of the Church*, vol. 20 [New York: n.p., 1953], ltr. 153, pp. 296-98.)

Similarly, Thomas Aquinas in the thirteenth century held that restitution was a matter of justice:

> Restitution establishes the equality of commutative justice. . . . Now this equalizing of things is impossible unless he that has less than his due receive what is lacking to him; and for this to be done, restitution must be made to the person from whom the thing has been taken. (*Summa Theologiae* [New York: Benzinger Brothers, 1973], part II-II, ques. 62, p. 1455.)

John Calvin in the sixteenth century agreed: "In whatever way, therefore, a man should have committed an offense, whereby another is made poorer, he is commanded to make good the loss." (*Commentary on the Four Last Books of Moses* [Grand Rapids, Mich.: Eerdmans, n.d.] 5:149.)

In colonial America, Jonathan Edwards considered restitution an obligation, and failure to make restitution, an *ongoing* sin:

> I exhort those who are conscious in themselves that they have wronged their neighbor to make restitution. This is a duty the obligation to which is exceedingly plain. . . . A man who hath gotten any thing from another wrongfully, goes on to wrong him every day that he neglects to restore it, when he has opportunity

to do it. The person injured did not only suffer wrong from the other when his goods were first taken from him, but he suffers new injustice from him all the while they are unjustly kept from him. (Henry Rogers, ed. *The Works of Jonathan Edwards*, rev. Edward Hickman [London: Ball, Arnold and Co., 1840], 2:226.)

[14]Albert Eglash, "Creative Restitution: Some Suggestions for Prison Rehabilitation Programs, "cited in Randy E. Barnett, "Restitution: A New Paradigm of Criminal Justice," in *Assessing the Criminal: Restitution, Retribution, and the Legal Process*, ed. Randy E. Barnett and John Nagel III (Cambridge, Mass.: Ballinger, 1977), p. 370.

Chapter 11: Reducing Crime

[1]The right to judge disputes between individuals has long been recognized as an important source of power. When Absalom was inciting Israel to join his rebellion against his father, David, one of his major promises was that he would decide justly all the matters that they brought to him. We can infer that the people felt that they did not have access to David to receive his judgments.

> Whenever anyone came with a complaint to be placed before the king for a decision, Absalom would call out to him, "What town are you from?" He would answer, "Your servant is from one of the tribes of Israel." Then Absalom would say to him, "Look, your claims are valid and proper, but there is no representative of the king to hear you." And Absalom would add, "If only I were appointed judge in the land! Then everyone who has a complaint or case could come to me and I would see that he gets justice." (2 Sam 15:2-4)

Perhaps this is why Solomon asked for wisdom in administering justice. He knew that this was a key to consolidating power. That certainly was the effect of his wisdom (1 Kings 3:16-28).

[2]Gresham M. Sykes and David Matza, "Techniques of Neutralization: A Theory of Delinquency," *American Sociological Review* 22 (December 1957): 664-70.

[3]Wilson and Herrnstein, *Crime and Human Nature*, p. 437.

[4]Ibid., p. 434.

[5]Ibid., p. 435.

[6]Ibid., p. 420.

[7]Robert Coles, "When Psychiatry Spurns Morality," *Washington Post* (18 August 1985).

[8]Ibid., p. 453.

[9]Anne M. Newton, "Prevention of Crime and Delinquency," *Criminal Justice Abstracts* (1978): 265.

[10]"Volunteer 'Watch' Programs Work to Reduce Crime," *Criminal Justice Newsletter*, 28 February 1983, p. 6.

[11]Mark W. Cannon, "Crime and the Decline of Values" (address to the Southwestern Judicial Conference, Sante Fe, New Mexico, 4 June 1981), p. 16.

[12]Joan Peterson and Emily Rovetch, *Partnerships for Neighborhood Crime Prevention* (Washington, D.C.: Government Printing Office, n.d.), p. 1.

[13]"Neighborhood Program Bulletin," (Washington, D.C.: Eisenhower Foundation, n.d.), p. 1.

[14]Peterson and Rovetch, *Partnerships*, p. 1.

[15]Ronald J. Troyer and R. Dean Wright, "Community Response to Crime: Two Middle-Class Anti-Crime Patrols," *Journal of Criminal Justice* 13 (1985): 232.

[16]Wesley G. Skogan and Michael G. Maxfield, *Coping with Crime* (Beverly Hills: Sage Pub., 1981), p. 234.

[17]George J. Washnis, *Citizen Involvement in Crime Prevention* (Lexington, Mass.: Lexington Books, 1976), p. 9.

[18]Quoted in Cannon, "Crime and the Decline of Values," p. 19.

[19]Smedes, *Mere Morality*, p. 1.

[20]While the relationship of religious involvement to disease is not our topic, Larson has found fascinating relationships. For example, regular church attenders appear to have lower suicide rates, lower blood pressure, fewer heart attacks and longer lives!

[21]Rodney Stark et al., "Rediscovering Moral Communities: Church Membership and Crime," in *Understanding Crime: Current Theory and Research*, ed. Travis Hirschi and Michael Gottfredson (Beverly Hills: Sage Pub., 1980), pp. 43-52.

[22]Steven Stack and Mary Jeanne Kanavy, "The Effect of Religion on Forcible Rape: A Structural Analysis," *Journal for the Scientific Study of Religion* 22, no. 1 (1983): 71.

[23]Cannon, "Crime and the Decline of Values," p. 6.

[24]F. Ivan Nye, *Family Relationships and Delinquent Behavior* (Westport, Conn.: Greenwood Press, 1958), p. 147.

[25]Rodney Stark et al., *Religion and Delinquency: The Ecology of a 'Lost' Relationship* (Seattle: University of Washington Center for Law and Justice, 1979), p. ii.

[26]Louis A. Cancellaro et al., "Religious Life of Narcotic Addicts," *Southern Medical Journal* 75, no. 10 (1982): 1166.

[27]David B. Larson and William P. Wilson, "Religious Life of Alcoholics," *Southern Medical Journal* 73, no. 6 (1980): 723.

[28]Jacqueline Johnson Jackson, "Marital Life among Aging Blacks," *The Family Coordinator* (January 1972), 2; John H. Scanzoni, *The Black Family in Modern Society: Patterns of Stability and Security* (Chicago: The University of Chicago Press, 1976), pp. 117, 120.

[29]Quoted in Joseph W. Rogers, *Why Are You Not a Criminal?* (Englewood Cliffs, N.J.: Prentice-Hall, 1977), pp. 116-17.

[30]Frank G. Goble and B. David Brooks, *The Case for Character Education* (Ottawa, Ill.: Green Hill, 1983), p. 46.

[31]Ibid., pp. 47-49, 120.

[32]Ibid.

[33]Newsletter of the Thomas Jefferson Research Center, September-October 1983, 1.

[34]Anatole France, *The Red Lilly*, trans. Winifred Stevens, *The Six Greatest Novels of Anatole France* (Garden City, N.Y.: Garden City Pub., n.d.), p. 837.

[35]Aleksandr I. Solzhenitsyn, *The Gulag Archipelago: Two* (New York: Harper and Row, 1975), p. 450.

Chapter 12: Responding to Crime

[1]This story, and the following information about the Earn-It program in Quincy, Massachusetts, is found in *The Earn-It Story* by Andrew Klein (Earn-It program, Quincy Court, 50 Chestnut Street, Quincy, MA 02169).

[2]For the theory, practical suggestions and evaluations of these programs, see Charles W. Colson and Daniel H. Benson, "Restitution as an Alternative to Imprisonment," *Detroit College of Law Review*, 1980, no. 2:523ff.; Galaway and Hudson, eds., *Offender Restitution;* Alan T. Harland et al., *A Guide to Restitution Programming* (Albany, N.Y.:

Criminal Justice Research Center, 1979); Alan T. Harland, *Monetary Remedies for the Victims of Crime: Assessing the Role of the Criminal Courts* (Albany, N.Y.: Criminal Justice Research Center, 1981); American Correctional Association, *Restitution Programming for Correctional Agencies: A Practical Guide* (Washington, D.C.: Law Enforcement Assistance Administration, 1981); Joe Hudson and Burt Galaway, eds., *Victims, Offenders and Alternative Sanctions* (Lexington, Mass.: Lexington Books, 1980); and Barnett and Hagel, eds., *Assessing the Criminal.*

[3]Steve Novack et al., "Victim and Offender Perceptions of the Fairness of Restitution and Community-Service Sanctions," in Hudson and Galaway, *Victims, Offenders and Alternative Sanctions*, p. 69.

[4]A United States Department of Justice study, based on surveys of victims of crime, concluded that few victims' losses are so costly as to preclude restitution by the offender, even considering the low income level of many defendants. The major limitations on extensive use of restitution include the rate of nonreporting of crimes, the low rates of arrest and conviction, and the very low or nonexistent wages paid to imprisoned offenders. Alan T. Harland, *Restitution to Victims of Personal and Household Crimes* (Washington, D.C.: Bureau of Justice Statistics, 1981).

[5]For a summary of these studies, see Joe Hudson and Burt Galaway, "A Review of the Restitution and Community-Service Sanctioning Research," in *Victims, Offenders and Alternative Sanctions*, ed. Hudson and Galaway, pp. 173ff.

[6]Ibid.; see also Colson and Benson, "Restitution as an Alternative to Imprisonment."

[7]See, for example, Scott H. Decker, "A Systematic Analysis of Diversion: Net Widening and Beyond," *Journal of Criminal Justice* 13 (1985): 207-16.

[8]When community service is to be used, as it should, as an alternative to prison for nonviolent offenders, the same issues are raised here as we discussed with restitution: courts often do not divert prison-bound offenders and instead order community service by offenders they would otherwise have simply placed on probation.

[9]Based on conversations with Stephen Donnelly, the Community Service Coordinator, and on two papers (unpublished): "Descriptive Analysis of the Performance of Community Service Probationers" by William E. Hemple and Stephen Donnelly, and "Community Service Orders in Federal Probation" by Stephen Donnelly.

[10]Novack et al., "Victim and Offender Perceptions," p. 69.

[11]Bradley M. Weiss, "The Cleveland Prosecutor Mediation Program," *NIJ Reports* SNI 190 (March 1985): 7.

[12]Ibid.

[13]Zehr, *Mediating the Victim-Offender Conflict*, p. 3.

[14]Mark Umbreit, *Crime and Reconciliation: Creative Options for Victims and Offenders* (Nashville: Abingdon Press, 1985), p. 101.

[15]Ibid., p. 100.

[16]Ibid., pp. 100-101.

[17]Ibid., p. 62.

[18]The following description and example are taken from an overview of the program completed after its first year of operation by David Mesaros, Mediation Coordinator, in a letter to me dated 3 June 1985.

[19]Mediation can also be initiated by the judge prior to sentencing.

[20]Margery Fry, "Justice for Victims," *London Observer*, 7 July 1957; rpt. *Journal of Public*

Law 8 (1959): 191-94.

[21]The following description of victim compensation and assistance programs comes from Christine Edmunds et al., *Campaign for Victims Rights, Practical guide: 1985* (Washington, D.C.: National Organization for Victim Assistance, 1985); William E. Hoelzel, "A Survey of 27 Victim Compensation Programs," *Judicature* 63, no. 10 (1980): 485ff.; Keith B. Richburg, "Justice Department Molds Program Aimed at Helping Crime Victims," *Washington Post*, 14 March 1985; and John A. Borden, "More States Compensating Victims of Violent Crime with Less Red Tape," *Los Angeles Times*, 12 April 1984.

[22]Gilbert Geis, "Victim Compensation and Restitution," in *Encyclopedia of Crime and Justice*, ed. Sanford Kadish (New York: Free Press, 1983), p. 1606.

[23]Richburg, "Justice Department Molds Program."

[24]Borden, "More States Compensating Victims of Violent Crime."

[25]Geis, "Victim Compensation and Restitution," pp. 1604ff.

[26]Chapter XIV of *The Comprehensive Crime Control Act of 1984*, Public Law #98-473, signed into law 12 October 1984.

[27]From Caroline Huntting of the National Organization for Victim Assistance, in a telephone conversation on 9 January 1986.

Chapter 13: Restraining Criminals

[1]Shaw, *Crime of Imprisonment*, p. 13.

[2]See Solomon, *Community Corrections*, pp. 9-10.

[3]Ibid., p. 12.

[4]Ibid., p. 13.

[5]Lawrence A. Greenfeld, *Probation and Parole, 1983* (Washington, D.C.: Bureau of Justice Statistics, 1984), p. 1.

[6]Mimi Cantwell and Lawrence A. Greenfeld, *Prisoners in 1983* (Washington, D.C.: Bureau of Justice Statistics, 1984), p. 1.

[7]Joan Petersilia et al., *Granting Felons Probation: Public Risks and Alternatives* (Santa Monica, Calif.: Rand Corporation, 1985).

[8]Ibid., pp. v-vi, 2.

[9]*Fifty* (probationers) was established by the American Correctional Association as the number for one officer to supervise. "[T]he current trend is . . . to determine appropriate caseload size [by] the types of probationers. For example, . . . 20 'maximum-supervision' cases; 'medium caseloads' might consist of 50 offenders; and 'low-supervision caseloads' might contain as many as 200." Ibid., p. 10.

[10]Ibid., pp. 64ff.

[11]Kathy Sawyer, "Tougher Probation May Help Georgia Clear Crowded Prisons," *Washington Post*, 16 August 1985.

[12]Camp and Camp, *The Corrections Yearbook*, p. 24.

[13]Bell and Thompson, *Attorney General's Task Force, Final Report*, p. 76.

[14]This is based on two reports issued by the Bureau of Justice Statistics, U.S. Department of Justice. *Examining Recidivism* (February 1985) showed that 16.1 per cent of the people sent to prison had no prior adult or juvenile conviction. *Prisons and Prisoners* (January 1982) showed that 7.9 per cent of the prisoners that year had a prior history of incarceration, but only as a juvenile.

[15]*Examining Recidivism,* p. 5, table 9.

[16]Mark Umbriet, *Reducing Prison Overcrowding through Community Corrections* (Michigan City, Ind.: Prisoner and Community Together, 1981), p. 3.

[17]Beck and Greenfeld, *Prisoners in 1984,* p. 3.

[18]Ibid., p. 7.

[19]Sawyer, "Tougher Probation May Help Georgia."

[20]Beck and Greenfeld, *Prisoners in 1984,* pp. 5ff.

[21]For a review of some of the excellent work in this area, see Goldfarb and Singer, *After Conviction;* Norval Morris, *The Future of Imprisonment* (Chicago: Univ. of Chicago Press, 1974); Kevin Wright, "Developing the Prison Environment Inventory," *Journal of Research in Crime and Delinquency* 22, no. 3 (1985): 257-77; and standards developed by the Commission on Accreditation Corrections, American Correctional Association, 4321 Hartwick Road, Suite L-208, College Park, MD 20740.

[22]These questions are adapted from my pamphlet, "A Call to Dialogue on Capital Punishment." Copies available at no charge from Justice Fellowship, P.O. Box 17181, Washington, DC 20041-0181.

[23]Deuteronomy 19 provides that two eyewitnesses were required for *any* case. But in those cases, the victim could be a witness. The purpose was to avoid a "swearing contest" between the victim and the accused, so the victim had to bring another witness.

But a murder victim cannot testify. So a murder case required at least two outside witnesses, instead of just one. And those witnesses were required to participate in the execution to underscore the seriousness of the charges, and to encourage truthfulness.

Jewish interpretation of this provision supports this view. They required the eyewitnesses not just to testify, but to agree in every detail *and* to testify that they warned the accused that he was about to commit a capital crime. (See Israel Kazis, "Judaism and the Death Penalty," in *The Death Penalty in America,* ed. Hugo A. Bedau [New York: Anchor Books, 1964], pp. 172-74.)

[24]Coker v. Georgia, 433 U.S. 584 (1977).

[25]Enmund v. Florida, 102 S.Ct. 3368 (1982).

[26]Furman v. Georgia, 408 U.S. 238 (1972).

[27]Woodson v. North Carolina, 428 U.S. 28 (1976).

[28]Jack Greenberg, "Capital Punishment as a System," *Yale Law Journal* 91 (April 1982): 919-20. A number of the cases he cites are pre-1972 cases, but there is evidence that this is still continuing. For example, Charlie Brooks was executed in 1982, in spite of serious doubts about his personal involvement in the murder. In fact, his *prosecutor* pleaded for his sentence to be commuted to life in prison because no one knew whether he or his codefendant (who was given a prison sentence in return for his testimony at trial) had actually committed the murder. (See Charles Colson, "That Execution Wasn't Painless," *Washington Post,* 11 December 1982).

[29]W. J. Bowers and G. L. Pierce, "Post-*Furman* Arbitrariness and Discrimination," *Crime and Delinquency* (October 1980): 600.

[30]Ibid., p. 575.

[31]Three studies have examined the impact of capital-punishment law revisions in seven states by comparing the resulting change in murder rates in those states with the rates

in surrounding states. For example, Oregon abolished capital punishment in the early 1960s. A study compared the homicide rate in Oregon with that of Washington, Idaho, California and Nevada (all of which have death penalty laws). Although the murder rates went up in all five states, they actually increased less in Oregon than in the other states.

This was also borne out in other studies. Only one of the seven states studied showed evidence that capital punishment deterred; in the others it had the opposite effect. (See E. J. Bowers and G. L. Pierce, "Deterrence or Brutalization: What Is the Effect of Executions?" *Crime and Delinquency* (October 1980): 462-63, n. 33.

I am aware of only one study which concluded that the death penalty does deter. It has been highly criticized for its methodology, and no researcher to date has been able to get the same results. Even capital punishment supporter Ernest van den Haag, after reviewing all the research, would only go so far as to say that the evidence was inconclusive. (See Ernest van den Haag and John Conrad, *The Death Penalty: A Debate* (New York: Plenum Press, 1983), p. 140.

[32]Neither Justice Fellowship nor Prison Fellowship Ministries has taken a position on this topic because of disagreement among board members and staff. However, as we have discussed the issue, we have discovered that it is possible to respect and learn from those who disagree with us. I encourage you to do the same.

Chapter 14: Where Do We Go from Here?
[1]Quoted in "In the Name of Justice," *The Justice Report,* summer 1985, p. 1.
[2]From a speech on 17 May 1985 in Indianapolis, reported in Charles Colson, "Living the Gospel: A Witness to the World," *The Justice Report,* summer 1985, p. 3.
[3]McHugh, *Christian Faith and Criminal Justice,* pp. 145ff.

Appendix B: How Much Restitution?
[1]Rushdooney, *Institutes of Biblical Law,* pp. 459-60.

General Index

Scripture Index